Game
In Good Taste

To Patty-Cake,
the wife of the best hunter
in Conifer, Colorado.
Merry Christmas!

Ann Gazacha

12-2-89

Game
In Good Taste

by
Ann Gorzalka

A feast of recipes
for wild game

HIGH PLAINS PRESS
GLENDO, WYOMING

Additional copies may be obtained
with the convenient order blanks at the back of the book.
Or write:
Game in Good Taste
High Plains Press
P.O. Box 123
Glendo, WY 82213
(307) 735-4370

Copyright © 1989
Ann Gorzalka
Printed in the United States of America
ISBN: 0-931271-11-8

*For my future hunters and cooks
Robert, Ivan, Brent,
Amy, Heather, Christy and Kyla.*

Acknowledgments

Special thanks is given to those who helped make this book possible. Not only did they share favorite recipes, but they gave encouragement and support when needed:

Opal Bohnsack, Sally Springer, Margaret Logan, Elsa Spear Byron, Sylvia Williams, Mary Buell, Diana McKenzie, Evelyn Williams, Helen Yetter, Kay Dockery, Sudie Cusenbury, Fredia Pearl, Bessie Green, Ida Kleineman, Betty Wood, Betty Lipson, and Rene Adams;

Hermie Belus, Dr. Earl Davis, Bernice Kobielusz, Elaine Wood, Helen Frazer, Beverly Gorzalka, Grace Mueller, Rebecca Barnhart, and John Stringer, winemaker at Stringer Orchards.

Also thanks to Linnet McGoodwin, Sheridan County Home Economist, and Mary Winger, University of Wyoming College of Agriculture.

Thanks to my hunters: Mike, Lonnie, Ron and Mike Jr., who bring home excellent meat which makes cooking a joy.

Ray A. Field, Professor of Animal Science and Extension Specialist in Foods and Nutrition, University of Wyoming, gave permission to use the findings of his many years' research in game animals. I thank him for his help.

A grateful thank you to those who tasted, especially my brother, Jim Williams, who tasted and never questioned during many trial runs.

Preface

Autumn in many parts of the country means hunting season. And to many of those who cook game meat it means echoing that old saying: "A hunter's pride is a cook's challenge."

If this strikes a chord, take heart, because with a little courage and know-how, the bounty brought home by your hunter can be a delicious taste treat.

Several years ago, I invited twenty dinner guests to enjoy a game buffet. Some of the game recipes in this book were served alongside one dish made with pork and one made with beef. When the meal was finished, I asked my guests to identify the dishes which contained domestic meat. Not one person could distinguish among the meats, even though some of the diners had eaten second, and even third, helpings.

That meal was the beginning. Each year I worked at creating new dishes using the variety of game meats and fowl that my hunters brought home. Now, the game buffets are an annual occasion and are eagerly anticipated by the invited guests.

I've come to think of game meat as Gourmet Meat to be savored and served with pride.

With the recipes in this book, I share the secrets of cooking game in good taste-- game you'll be proud to serve at special luncheons, formal sit-down dinners, buffets, potlucks and family picnics.

I've also included vegetables, salads, breads and desserts recipes which seem to especially enhance game meat.

So let your imagination go; meet the challenge of creating delicious meals with hunters' bounty--meals fit for any occasion. You, too, will soon think of game meat as Gourmet Meat.

Contents

Meats
11

Jerky & Sausage
53

Vegetables & Salads
79

Hot Breads
109

Desserts
127

Field Care & Aging
149

Index
155

Ann Gorzalka has been cooking game meats, birds and fish for twenty-five years. As word of her expertise spread, she has been asked to teach classes on the preparation and cooking of game meats in colleges and special sessions throughout the West.

The author writes a regularly appearing cooking column in a monthly Wyoming magazine. She is also the author of a non-fiction book *The Saddlemakers of Sheridan, Wyoming*.

*Artwork on Page 150
by Evelyn Williams.*

Meats

Meats

Within these pages you will find ways to prepare game meat that will result in praise for the cook and pride for the hunter. You'll find recipes which turn game into dishes fit for any occasion--recipes which truly turn game meat into Gourmet Meat.

I believe the most common mistake in cooking game is to smother it in garlic and onions. These vegetables complement game meat only when cooked separately and added later to the cooked meat.

Dairy products, butter, sour cream and cheese are delicious with game meat. The addition of dairy products makes the difference between an ordinary dish and one that brings rave reviews from those lucky diners.

Don't be afraid to experiment with herbs and spices; fruits (fresh or dried) also are good when used in combination with Gourmet Game.

Remember, not only is game one of nature's most healthy foods, it also has higher amounts of usable protein than domestic meat. It is lower in calories and fat, which makes it excellent fare for people on restricted diets.

Of course, the first considerations in the preparation of subtly-flavored game begins before the cook takes possession. The first and most important step in providing good game meat is proper dressing in the field. The second decision involves how long to age the meat before freezing. Field care and aging are discussed in the final section of this book and I urge you to read the section carefully. Even if your hunter is experienced in these matters, please review the section.

When you are ready to prepare a meal using your game meat, first wash the fresh or thawed meat in cool water several times. Drain the meat or pat it dry. Cut away any parts which won't be eaten.

If more some reason, the meat is more strong flavored that you'd like, place the meat into a combination of 1/2 cup of bottled lemon juice to one quart of cold water. Let it marinate in the refrigerator for at least two hours. Many people prefer to leave the meat in the marinade overnight. Drain the meat before using it.

Some of these recipes don't specify a particular variety of game meat; they simply call for Gourmet Meat or Gourmet Grind. This is because they work equally well with elk, deer, antelope, or other wild game meat. These recipes are also delicious when made with domestic meat.

If no one cut of meat is called for, it is because several different cuts are suitable. Experiment a little to see which cuts you prefer in each recipe.

Special Menus

Holiday Buffet

Wild Smoked Turkey, page 49
Frozen Cranberry Salad, page 104
Sweet Potato Surprise, page 84
Molded Mixed Vegetables, page 101
Herbed Rolls, page 119
Pineapple Fudge, page 129

Harvest Feast

Moist Gourmet Roast, page 27
Potato Dumplings, page 83
Carrot Surprise, page 91
Fruit Slaw, page 103
Kay's Cornmeal Buns, page 120
Mincemeat Stuffed Apples, page 146

New Year's Supper

Pheasant in Sour Cream, page 44
Cucumber-Pineapple Salad, page 106
Yam Bread, page 116
Cherry Brandied Apples, page 134

Royal Stuffed Steak

Ingredients:

    1 slice round steak, 1-inch thick
    5 Tbsp. butter, divided
    1 Tbsp. onion, minced
    2 cups dried bread crumbs
    1/2 lb. pork sausage
    1/2 tsp. poultry seasoning
    salt and pepper to taste
    1/4 cup milk
    1/2 cup chopped walnuts
    potatoes and carrots, if desired

Cook and drain pork sausage; set aside. Saute minced onion in two tablespoons of the butter. Add bread crumbs, sausage, poultry seasoning, salt, pepper, milk and walnuts. Mix until moistened.

Pound round steak until it is thin. Spread sausage mixture over steak. Roll steak, jellyroll style, and tie with string or fasten with toothpicks. Brown rolled meat in a heavy pan with three tablespoons of the butter. Cook on top of stove over low heat, turning to brown on all sides. Add water as needed to keep meat from burning. Continue cooking and turning the roll for one hour. Potatoes and carrots may be added during the last 45 minutes of cooking time.

MUSHROOM GRAVY

2 T. butter
3 T. flour
2 cups canned mushrooms with juice

Melt butter in fry pan. Add flour. Cook until bubbly, but do not brown. Add the mushrooms and juice, all at once, to the butter-flour mixture. Cook, stirring until thickened. Add more water if needed. Pour over the steak roll just before serving.

Chicken Fried Steak

This is a failproof beginning dish for novice game cooks.

Japanese breading can be found in the oriental food section of most supermarkets.

For a guest-pleasing change of pace, serve strips of chicken-fried meat as hors d'oeuvers. Arrange the strips on a serving dish around a small bowl of horseradish dip.

TWO HORSERADISH DIPS

#1. Mix together:
1 cup catsup
2 T. Worcestershire sauce
2 T. hot horseradish

#2. Mix together:
1 cup sour cream
1 T. chopped green pepper
4 T. horseradish
salt & pepper

Ingredients:
- **6 pieces boneless steak** (minute steaks works well)
- **cornstarch**
- **1 cup vegetable oil**
- **2 eggs, beaten**
- **1 1/2 cups crumbs** (cracker crumbs, dried bread crumbs or Japanese breading mix)

As always, begin with steaks which have been washed in cool water and drained dry.

1. Dust six steaks with cornstarch.
2. Dip meat into beaten eggs and roll in crumbs. Cracker crumbs or dried bread crumbs work well, but Japanese breading mix is excellent because it adheres to the meat and browns more slowly.
3. Drop prepared steaks into fry pan of hot oil, deep enough to cover them. Cook about three minutes on each side; more if steaks are very thick. Breading should be brown, but do not overcook meat.

The flavor and goodness of meat cooked this way can stand deliciously alone. Or try serving it with catsup, chili sauce, or barbecue sauce.

Tarragon Cube Steak

Ingredients:
- **6 pieces cube steak**
- **3/4 cup salad dressing**
- **1/4 cup lemon juice**
- **1 Tbsp. tarragon**
- **salt & pepper, if desired**

Make a marinade by mixing the salad dressing, lemon juice, tarragon and salt and pepper. Pour above mixture over six pieces of cube steak. Refrigerate overnight.

Place marinated meat on rack in broiling pan. Brush occasionally with marinade while broiling.

Cube steak is also known as minute steak.

Of course, you can make your own cube steak by pounding pieces of boneless steak with a meat pounder or another heavy utensil.

Steak Gourmet Delight

Frozen breaded onion rings may be found in the freezer department of your grocery store.

Ingredients:

8 pieces steak
1/4 cup butter
Salt and pepper
1 cup tomato sauce
3/4 cup sour cream
1/2 cup grated parmesan cheese
1/4 tsp. oregano
1 cup mushrooms, sliced
Breaded onion rings, frozen

Brown eight serving-sized pieces of steak in butter. Transfer steaks to a baking dish. Salt and pepper to taste.

Combine tomato sauce, sour cream, parmesan cheese, oregano and mushrooms. Pour over browned meat. Arrange frozen breaded onion rings over top. Bake at 350 degrees for 40 minutes.

Rolls Roices

Ingredients:
- **6 pieces round steak**
- **1/2 cup carrots**
- **1 medium potato**
- **1 cup sauerkraut**
- **salt and pepper to taste**
- **1/4 cup butter**
- **1/2 cup water**
- **1 Tbsp. Worcestershire sauce**

Pound six serving-sized portions of steak until thin. Grate carrots and potatoes; mix with sauerkraut. Add salt and pepper to taste. Spoon two tablespoons of vegetables onto each steak. Roll and secure with toothpicks.

Heat butter in fry pan. Add meat-and-vegetable rolls and brown on all sides.

After meat is browned, add 1/2 cup of water and Worcestershire sauce to fry pan.

Cover tightly and simmer for one hour. Add water as needed. Thicken gravy and serve over Rolls Roices.

To thicken gravy for this recipe I usually use :
1 T. of flour or cornstarch to
2 cups of water.

1. Put the flour or cornstarch in a small, deep container.
2. Gradually add water, stirring continually until a smooth paste is made.
3. Then gradually add tablespoonfuls of the hot meat juice to the paste and blend.
4. Return the flour/meat juice mixture to the pan and simmer for two or three minutes until gravy reaches the desired consistency.

Steak and Honey Sauce

Ingredients:

- 6 small steak pieces
- 1 Tbsp. grated ginger root
- 3/4 cup lemon juice, divided
- 1 tsp. paprika
- 1/2 cup butter, divided
- 1/2 cup honey
- flour
- salt and pepper

Store grated ginger root in freezer in one teaspoon amounts to use as needed. It keeps well up to three months.

In a shallow pan, combine ginger root, 1/2 cup of the lemon juice, and paprika. Add steaks to mixture and marinate for two hours in refrigerator.

In a large fry pan, melt 1/4 cup of the butter. Roll steaks in salted and peppered flour and brown in butter. Watch carefully to prevent burning. When browned, lower heat and continue cooking until done.

Mix the other 1/4 cup butter with the remaining 1/4 cup lemon juice and the honey. Pour this sauce over meat and simmer for ten minutes.

Caramelized Chops with Walnuts & Raisins

Ingredients:

- 4 chops , 1-inch thick
- 1/2 cup sugar
- 1/2 cup cider vinegar
- 6 Tbsps. vegetable oil
- 4 Tbsps. butter
- 1/2 cup walnuts, coarsely chopped
- 1/2 cup raisins
- 1/4 cup dry sherry

Chops are cut from the loin and usually have a bone in them. When these same cuts are boned, they are referred to as boneless top loin steaks, boneless sirloin steaks, tenderloin steaks or roast.

Combine sugar and vinegar; stir until sugar is dissolved. Marinate meat in sugar/vinegar mixture for 20 minutes in refrigerator.

Heat vegetable oil in heavy fry pan until hot. Add chops; fry over high heat on both sides until they caramelize. Watch closely to prevent burning.

In another fry pan, heat butter and add walnuts. Saute.

Remove chops from pan. Add sherry to drippings. Cook over high heat until liquid is reduced to four tablespoons. Lower heat and add nuts and the butter in which they were cooked. Add raisins and meat. Simmer until chops are tender.

This is great served over rice.

Chops in Wine Sauce

Ingredients:
6 chops
3 Tbsps. butter
1 cup white wine
1/2 cup apple jelly
flour
salt and pepper

For an eye-pleasing serving platter, garnish with baked apple halves.

Flour chops; salt and pepper to taste; then brown in butter. Place browned chops in baking dish.

Combine and mix white wine and apple jelly. Pour sauce over the chops. Bake in 325 degree oven for 30 minutes.

Chops and Cabbage

Ingredients:
- 6 chops
- 3 Tbsps. butter
- flour
- salt and pepper
- 1/4 cup water
- 3 whole cloves
- 1 small bay leaf
- 1/2 tsp. sweet basil
- one medium cabbage, chopped
- 1 cup chopped apple
- 1/4 cup chopped green pepper
- 1/4 cup chopped onion
- 1/4 cup brown sugar
- 1 1/2 tsps. cornstarch
- 2 Tbsps. vinegar
- 2 Tbsps. water

Dredge chops in flour, seasoned with salt and pepper, and brown in butter in a large fry pan. Add water, cloves, bay leaf and basil to chops. Cover and simmer for 15 minutes. Remove chops; discard cloves and bayleaf.

To remaining meat liquid in fry pan, add cabbage, apple, green pepper, onion and salt.

Combine brown sugar and cornstarch; stir in vinegar and water. Pour sugar/vinegar mixture over cabbage and mix well. Place chops on top. Cover; simmer 25 minutes.

Glazed Chops

Try serving this over a can of Chinese noodles.

For another serving suggestion, tiny new potatoes and pearl onions in cream sauce make a fine accompaniment for this dish.

First, peel and cook potatoes and onions. Then add this cream sauce.

CREAM SAUCE

3 T. butter
1 1/2 T. flour
2 cups milk
1/2 t. dry mustard
1 t. seasoned salt
1/4 t. pepper

Cook butter and flour together until bubbly. Add milk, dry mustard, salt and pepper. Cook and stir until thickened. Add cooked, peeled potatoes and onions. Heat through.

Ingredients:
  6 chops or steaks
  3 Tbsps. butter
  2/3 cup orange marmalade
  1/4 cup dry, white wine
  1/4 tsp. grated ginger root
  1/2 cup slivered almonds

Brown chops or steaks in butter. Place browned meat in bake-and-serve dish.

Mix together marmalade, wine, ginger root and almonds. Pour over chops.

Bake in moderate over (325 degrees) for 30 minutes.

Gourmet Parmesan

Ingredients:

- 2 cups sliced meat
- 1/4 cup butter
- 3 Tbsps. paprika
- 1 tsp. Italian Seasoning
- 1 cup catsup
- 1 1/2 cups water
- 1/4 cup grated parmesan cheese
- salt and pepper to taste
- 2 cups unpeeled zucchini chunks
- 1/2 cup green pepper chunks
- 1 medium onion, chopped

Cut meat into thin slices about one inch long. Brown meat strips in butter.

Add paprika, Italian Seasoning, catsup, water, parmesan cheese and salt and pepper to meat. Simmer 15 minutes; add water as needed, 1/4 cup at a time.

To the meat mixture, add zucchini, peppers, and onions. Continue to simmer until vegetables are tender crisp. Add more cheese if desired.

Freshly grated parmesan has a much more delicate flavor than that you buy in a can. I think the bonus in subtle flavor makes it worthwhile to grate your own.

When served over cooked, drained spaghetti, this dish makes a delicious change of pace meal.

I make this recipe in large quantities, when the zucchini is large and plentiful, and freeze it in meal-sized containers. If using large zucchini, they should be peeled. To serve after freezing, place the frozen casserole in a suitable saucepan and simmer over low heat until sauce thickens, about 30 minutes.

Noodles & Strips in Sour Cream

Corn on the cob is a perfect complement to this dish.

Ingredients:

1 lb. fresh meat
1 8-ounce package noodles
1/4 cup butter
flour seasoned with salt & pepper
1 1/2 cups sour cream
1 Tbsp. Worcestershire sauce
1 Tbsp. minced onion
1 tsp. salt
1/8 tsp. pepper
dash of hot pepper sauce
1 Tbsp. blue cheese, crumbled
green pepper rings

First, cook and drain noodles.

Wash and pat dry meat. Cut it into short, narrow strips. Dredge in flour seasoned with salt and pepper. Brown in fry pan in butter.

Mix together sour cream, Worcestershire sauce, minced onion, salt, pepper, hot sauce and blue cheese. Add this mixture to cooked noodles.

Arrange one-half of noodle mixture in a baking dish. Layer meat strips on top. Cover with remaining noodles and top with green pepper rings.

Bake for 30 minutes in 375 degree oven.

Two Delicious Roasts

MOIST ROAST PERFECTION

Ingredients:

1 roast, any size
2 Tbsp. butter
1 pkg. beef stew seasoning mix
flour, salt and pepper

Wash roast in cool water and pat dry. Salt and pepper roast; then in butter. Place meat in deep baking dish and coat it with stew seasoning mix.

Next make a thick paste of flour and water; spread it over roast until meat is covered with paste.

Cook in 350 degree oven, allowing 30 minutes per pound. Remove flour shell before serving.

Good with spicy apple butter.

ANOTHER MOIST ROAST

Ingredients:

1 roast
2 Tbsps. butter
1 pkg. beef stew seasoning mix
2 cups water
potatoes and carrots, if desired

Wash meat and pat dry. Brown roast in butter in a heavy pan. Coat meat with one package of seasoning mix and add water. Place tight-fitting lid on pan. Simmer on top of stove until tender. Add water as needed. About 30-45 minutes before serving, add potatoes and carrots. Serve meat juices over meat and vegetables.

A delicious meal in a pot.

Curried Chopped Roast and Vegetables

A sourdough biscuit recipe which is good with this dish can be found on p. 113.

A recipe for a good biscuit mix is on page 37.

Ingredients:

    2 cups cooked roast, chopped
    1/4 cup butter
    2 1/2 tsps. curry powder
    1 small green pepper, chopped
    1/4 cup onion, chopped
    1/4 cup grated carrot
    3 Tbsps. flour
    salt and pepper to taste
    2 cups chicken bouillon
    1 tsp. grated lemon peel

In fry pan, melt butter. Add curry powder; heat and stir.

Add pepper, carrot, and onion. Cook until tender crisp.

Blend in flour and add salt and pepper to taste.

Add chicken bouillon. Cook a few minutes before adding chopped, cooked roast (leftover is great) and grated lemon peel. After roast and vegetables are heated through, serve over biscuits.

Luncheon Salad

Ingredients:

    1 cup coarsely-ground cooked roast
    3/4 cup salad dressing
    3 hard-boiled eggs, chopped
    1 Tbsp. minced onion
    1 cup chopped celery
    1/2 cup minced green pepper
    1 Tbsp. lemon juice
    1 cube beef bouillon
    1 3-ounce pkg. lemon gelatin
    1 cup boiling water

Mix together roast, salad dressing, eggs, onion, celery, green pepper, and lemon juice.

Dissolve bouillon cube and gelatin in boiling water. Cool before adding to meat mixture.

Place in a 9-by-13 inch Pyrex baking dish; chill. Cut into squares and serve.

This is especially good served with coleslaw.

For a special luncheon, serve this with relishes in a festive ice bowl.

ICE BOWL
Fill a 2-quart bowl partially full of water colored with food coloring. Add non-toxic plastic or fresh flowers. Fill a smaller plastic bowl with cold water and center it inside the 2-quart bowl. Weight down smaller bowl by placing a plastic glass of cold water into the bowl. Place filled bowls and glass on a cookie sheet and level it in freezer. When water is frozen, dip bowls in warm water until the two bowls come free of the ice, leaving a bowl-shaped ice form. Return ice bowl to freezer for an hour before filling.

*   Just before serving, line ice bowl with lettuce, fill it, and place it on a serving dish lined with a paper doily.*

Smoothly Elegant Mousse

This is a perfect luncheon entree.

To soften gelatin, empty package into small pan. Add 1/2 cup broth and let set 5 minutes. Then place pan over low heat, stirring constantly until mixture is syrupy. Do not boil.

Gelatin may also be softened in the microwave. Use microwave-proof container. Cook on full power for 30 seconds or until gelatin is dissolved and syrupy.

Evaporated milk whips more readily if you use this method: Pour 1 cup of evaporated milk into a freezer-proof bowl and place in the freezer for 15-25 minutes, or until ice crystals begin to form around the sides. Whip just before adding to the recipe.

Ingredients:
   1 pkg. unflavored gelatin
   1 1/2 cups chicken broth, divided
   2 Tbsps. chopped celery
   1 Tbsp. minced green pepper
   1 Tbsp. minced onion
   1 cup coarsely ground, cooked roast
   1 Tbsp. sliced, stuffed olives
   1 cup evaporated milk, whipped

Soften gelatin in 1/2 cup of the broth; dissolve over low heat. Remove from heat. Add remaining one cup of chicken broth.

Chill until slightly thickened. Fold in ground roast, celery, green pepper, onion, olives and whipped milk. Place in a one-quart mold and chill until firm.

Just before serving, unmold and place on a serving tray. Garnish with spiced apple rings or cranberry jelly slices.

Or for a special luncheon, serve the mousse in a festive ice bowl. The instructions for making an ice bowl are on page 29. Place greens in ice bowl, and unmold mousse onto the greens. Garnish with pimento strips, green olives, and radishes.

Stuffed Crepes Supreme

Ingredients for crepes:
- **1 cup flour**
- **1/4 cup cornmeal**
- **3 eggs**
- **1 1/4 cups milk**
- **1/4 tsp. salt**
- **2 Tbsps. melted butter**
- **1/4 cup brandy**

Combine flour, cornmeal and salt. Add eggs and melted butter, mixing to remove lumps. Slowly stir in milk and brandy until batter is the consistency of thin cream. Let batter rest one hour before cooking.

Ladle one tablespoon of batter into buttered six-inch skillet over medium-high heat, tilting pan so that batter covers large surface. When edges begin to brown, turn. When lightly browned, remove from heat.

Ingredients for filling:
- **3 cups shredded, cooked meat**
- **1 cup sour cream**
- **1/2 cup chopped green chiles**
- **1 cup grated cheddar cheese**

Arrange about one tablespoonful of meat on each crepe. Roll and place in bake-and-serve dish. Top with sour cream, chiles, and cheese. Bake in 375 degree oven for 25 minutes.

This recipe makes about 12-15 crepes. I plan to serve two or three crepes for each person.

This is delightful when served with Tomato Pudding.

TOMATO PUDDING

2 cups stewed tomatoes
1/2 cup brown sugar
1/4 t. basil
1/4 t. oregano
2 cups fresh, white bread cubes
2 1/2 T. melted butter

Combine tomatoes, basil, oregano and brown sugar in saucepan and bring to a boil. Boil for 5 minutes. Place bread cubes in buttered, one-quart casserole dish. Top with melted butter; then add tomato mixture. Bake in 350 degree oven for 30 minutes.

Deep-Fried Turnovers

These turnovers are wonderful when served with Stringer's Wild Plum Dressing. I was able to get the wild plum dressing recipe when I was visiting Stringer's Orchard in Oregon. When Mr. Stringer, the winemaker there, heard that I enjoyed cooking, he gave me a jar of wild plum jam so that I could try the dressing recipe. It is truly delightful.

Ingredients:

2 cups, plus 3 Tbsps. flour, divided
1/2 tsp. salt
2/3 cup, plus 3 Tbsps. softened butter, divided
1/3 cup cold water
3 Tbsps. onion, chopped
1 cup chicken broth or bouillon
2 eggs, separated
4 cups ground, cooked game roast
1 tsp. dry mustard
1/2 tsp. pepper
3 Tbsps. sour cream

Pastry:
Blend two cups of the flour, salt, 2/3 cup of the softened butter, and water together into a dough. Wrap in plastic wrap and chill overnight.

Filling:
Cook onions in three tablespoons of the butter until clear. Add the remaining three tablespoons of flour and cook until bubbly. Add chicken broth and cook, stirring constantly, until thickened. In a separate bowl, beat egg yolks, gradually adding some of the hot mixture to yolks while stirring. Add egg mixture to remaining gravy. Add meat, mustard, pepper and sour cream.

(recipe continued on next page)

(turnover recipe, continued)

To make turnovers:
Take dough from refrigerator one hour before using. Let set at room temperature, but do not let dough get too warm. Roll dough into circle 1/8-inch thick and 13-inches round. Cut six-inch circles from dough, rerolling scraps of dough as needed, until you have eight circles.

Spoon two tablespoons of meat filling into center of each round of dough. Dampen edges of round with water and fold pastry over the filling to make half-circles. Pinch, or use fork prongs, to seal pastry edges.

Deep-fry filled turnovers for six to eight minutes each, turning occasionally so that they brown evenly. Drain in paper-layered pan. Serve with Stringer's Wild Plum Dressing.

STRINGER'S WILD PLUM DRESSING

1 cup Stringer's Wild Plum Jam
3/4 cup sour cream

Mix together well and serve over hot turnovers.

This dressing is delicious on these meat turnovers, and it is also good on dessert turnovers.

Gourmet Grind Seasoning

The following combination of ingredients seems to improve the taste, texture and moistness of ground game-burger when added to the meat and allowed to marinate several hours or overnight. I call this seasoned meat Gourmet Grind; it is suitable for any meal--even the most elegant.

This combination of seasonings added to ground game meat makes an excellent all-purpose burger which I call Gourmet Grind.

Gourmet Grind Seasoning will flavor and tenderize game meat which is somewhat tough or dry. I also suggest, to prevent rancid-tasting meat, that no fat or tallow be added during the grinding process. A suitable amount of fat or tallow should be added just before cooking.

GOURMET GRIND SEASONING

2 lbs. ground game meat
1/2 cup lemon juice
1/2 cup corn oil
2 Tbsps. Worcestershire sauce
1 Tbsp. dry mustard
1 tsp. dill weed (fresh or dry)

Combine and mix well. When frying meat seasoned with Gourmet Grind, quite a bit of liquid will form, but it will cook away, leaving the meat brown and delicious.

Use ground burger flavored with Gourmet Grind Seasoning in any recipe calling for burger.

Jalapenos Treat

Ingredients
> 2 lbs. prepared Gourmet Grind (p.34)
> 1 can refried beans
> 3/4 cup sour cream
> salt and pepper to taste
> 1 small jar jalapenos cheese spread

On a sheet of heavy foil, pat ground meat into a rectangle 1/4-inch thick. See page 34 for Gourmet Grind recipe

Mix refried beans, sour cream, cheese spread, and salt and pepper. Spread over meat.

Roll as for jelly roll, making foil work for you. When rolled, secure foil around meat.

Place in baking pan in 350 degree oven. Bake one hour. Let cool 15 minutes before slicing. Serve with your favorite sauce or salsa.

Remember: Gourmet Grind is seasoned game-burger. See p. 34 for seasoning recipe.

Jalapenos cheese spread comes in mild, medium and hot. I use mild in this recipe, but you may prefer a more spicy taste.

EASY SALSA

2 T. salad oil
2 T. diced onion
1 clove minced garlic
1/2 t. salt
1 dash hot sauce
*1 cup stewed
    tomatoes*
*1 small can diced
    green chiles*

Heat oil and cook onions and garlic until soft. Add remaining ingredients. Simmer for five minutes.

Sour Cream Chili Bake

FLOUR TORTILLAS

Mix together:
4 cups flour
1 t. salt

Add in small amounts while mixing:
1/2 cup shortening
1 1/4 cups warm water

Knead the dough thoroughly; it should be smooth and elastic. Form 20 dough balls. Using hands, form a circle of dough and flatten into a large circle with a rolling pin. Place in hot, ungreased frying pan. Cook until bubbles form. Turn and cook the other side. Put hot tortillas in a tightly covered container. Store in a cool, dry place. Plastic bags can be used for storage.

Ingredients:
1 lb. prepared Gourmet Grind (p.34)
2 cups cooked kidney beans, drained
1 pkg. chili seasoning mix
1 cup tomato sauce
1/2 cup water
3/4 cup cubed Velveeta cheese,
1/2 cup shredded Velveeta cheese
1 cup sour cream
flour tortillas, prepared or selfmade

Brown one pound of prepared Gourmet Grind (see recipe on p. 34). Drain.

Add kidney beans, chili seasoning, tomato sauce, water, sour cream, and the 3/4 cup of cubed cheese to the meat and mix well.

Line baking dish with flour tortillas (buy prepared ones or make your own wih the recipe in the sidebar). Fill dish with chili mixture. Sprinkle additional 1/2 cup of shredded cheese over top of casserole and bake in 375 degree oven for 30 minutes.

Gourmet Tart

Ingredients:

    1 cup grated cheddar cheese
    1 cup Gourmet Grind, cooked and
           drained (see p. 34)
    3 eggs
    1 1/2 cups milk
    1 tsp. minced onion
    1 tsp. dry mustard
    1/2 cup biscuit mix (recipe at right)
    butter
    chili powder
    salt and pepper

Butter a 9-inch pie plate. Sprinkle bottom and sides of pie plate lightly with chili powder.

Add cheese and cooked, drained burger in alternating layers.

Beat together eggs, milk, minced onion, dry mustard, biscuit mix (use prepared mix or the recipe at right). Add salt and pepper to taste. Pour this mixture over the meat/cheese layers.

Bake in 325 degree oven until set, approximately 30 to 40 minutes.

BISCUIT MIX

8 1/2 cups flour, white or wheat
3 T. baking powder
1 T. salt
2 tsps. cream of tartar
1 1/2 t. baking soda
1 3/4 cups powdered milk
1 T sugar
2 1/2 cups shortening

Sift together dry ingredients. Cut in shortening until mixture resembles cornmeal. Store in airtight container. Yield 13 cups.

Surprise Meatballs

This is good served over cooked rice to which chopped cashews have been added.

These make fine hors d'oeuvres. Make rather small meatballs. Arrange them on a serving dish with a toothpick in each one. The sauce can be placed in a small bowl and set in the center of the meatball dish,

Ingredients:
- 1 lb. prepared Gourmet Grind (p.34)
- 1 egg
- 1 cup dry bread crumbs
- 1/4 tsp. salt
- 1/4 tsp. pepper
- 2 Tbsps. butter
- 1 can crushed pineapple, save juice
- 1 can cranberry sauce
- 1/2 cup bottled barbecue sauce
- 1 Tbsp. cornstarch
- 1/4 cup water

Add egg, bread crumbs, and salt and pepper to the seasoned Gourmet Grind burger. Form meat into small balls; fry in butter until brown. Drain.

Drain pineapple, saving the juice. Mix together pineapple, cranberry sauce, and barbecue sauce. Pour sauce over meatballs.

Mix together cornstarch, water, and pineapple juice. Pour this mixture onto meat balls and cook, stirring until mixture thickens.

Gourmet Stew

Ingredients:
- 1 lb. stew meat
- flour
- 3 Tbsps. butter
- 3 1/2 cups cold water, divided
- 1/2 tsp. pepper
- 1 tsp. seasoned salt
- 1/2 tsp. chili powder
- 1 tsp. parsley
- 1/2 tsp. basil
- 1/2 cup diced celery
- 1 cup diced carrots
- 1 cup diced potatoes
- 1 small onion
- 2 Tbsps. cornstarch

This is extra good with hot bread. Kay's Cornmeal Buns (p. 120) are my favorites.

Corn Cups (p. 125) are delicous when filled with this stew.

Cut stew meat into bite-sized pieces. Dredge in flour and brown in butter.

Celery likes to drink. Keep celery in a glass container of water in the bottom of the refrigerator--a wide-mouthed jar works nicely.

Add three cups of the water, pepper, salt, chili powder, parsley, basil and celery. Bring to boil. Lower heat and simmer one hour. Stir occasionally, adding water if needed.

Add carrots, potatoes, and onion. Cook until tender, about an hour.

Add 1/2 cup of water to cornstarch. Blend and add to the stew. Stir until thickened.

Layered Taco Teaser

This is excellent fare for a carry-in supper as well as a delicious entree for a Mexican buffet.

Ingredients:
- 2 lbs. Gourmet Grind (see p.34)
- 2 Tbsps. butter
- 1 pkg. taco seasoning mix
- 1 cup water
- 1 cup cream style corn
- 1/2 tsp. pepper
- 1 pkg. flour tortillas
- 1 3/4 cup grated cheddar cheese
- 1 3/4 cups nacho Dorito chips
- 1/2 cup chopped green chiles
- 1 cup sour cream
- 1/2 tsp. salt
- 1/2 cup sliced, black olives
- 3/4 cup diced, fresh tomato

Brown seasoned Gourmet Grind burger in butter. Drain off fat; divide meat in half. Add to half the meat in the fry pan: taco seasoning, water, corn, and pepper. Mix well and bring to a boil.

Line a 9-by-13 inch baking dish with flour tortillas. Spread meat mixture over them. Sprinkle with 3/4 cup of the grated cheddar, then 3/4 cup of the crushed chips. Bake at 350 degrees for 30 minutes.

The finished casserole looks pretty garnished with avocado slices. Sprinkle lemon juice on the avocado to keep the slices fresh appearing.

Add chiles, sour cream and salt to remaining burger to make second layer. Mix well and spread over baked layer. Top with one cup crushed Doritos, olives, tomato, and remaining one cup of cheese. Return to oven and bake 15 minutes.

Meximix

Ingredients:
>   **1 lb. Gourmet Grind** (see p. 34)
>   **1/2 cup chopped green pepper**
>   **1 pkg. taco mix, divided**
>   **2 cups kidney beans**
>   **1 cup grated cheddar, divided**
>   **1/2 cup cornmeal**
>   **2 cups water**
>   **1/4 cup butter**
>   **2 eggs**
>   **salt to taste**

The flavor of this one-dish meal really comes to life with the bite of a tart salad such as the Grapefruit and Avocado Salad on page 102.

Brown seasoned Gourmet Grind burger (recipe on page 34) and drain.

Add green pepper, one-half of taco seasoning mix, kidney beans, and one-half of cheese. Place in a 10-by-13 inch baking dish.

To prepare topping, mix cornmeal and water in a saucepan. Bring to a boil, stirring constantly. Remove from heat and add butter, the remaining 1/2 cup of cheese, and salt to taste. Cool.

Add eggs and remaining one-half package of taco seasoning mix. Blend together well and pour over meat mixture.

Bake in 375 degree oven for 35 minutes. Serves eight.

South of the Border Individual Quiches

QUICHE CRUST

*1/2 cup butter
1 3-oz pkg.
cream cheese
1/2 cup cornmeal
1 1/2 cups flour
1/2 t. salt*

Soften butter and cream cheese before working with them. Then cream them together. Combine flour, cornmeal and salt. Add dry ingredients gradually to the butter/cheese mixture. Continue stirring until mixed.

Line greased muffin tins with dough, forming a cup in each tin. Makes 12 individual quiche shells.

Filled quiches can be baked ahead , then cooled and frozen. Remove them from freezer one hour before serving and leave at room temperature for 30 minutes. Turn pan upside down and tap until quiches fall out. Bake at 325 for 30 minutes or until hot.

Prepare quiche shells with recipe at left. Do not bake yet.

Ingredients for filling:
- 1 lb. Gourmet Grind (see p. 34)
- 3 Tbsps. butter
- 2 cups refried beans
- 1 cup sour cream
- 2 eggs, beaten
- 1 cup shredded cheddar cheese
- 1 tsp. chili powder
- salt to taste

Brown seasoned Gourmet Grind in butter. Drain and combine with other ingredients. Mix well.

Ladle mixture into unbaked quiche shells. Bake in 350 degree oven for 30 minutes. Serve with cheese sauce on the side.

Ingredients for cheese sauce:
- 3 Tbsps. butter
- 2 Tbsps. flour
- 1 1/2 tsps. dry mustard
- 2 cups milk
- 1 small jar Jalapenos-flavored cheese spread (mild)

Melt butter; add flour, mustard and milk. Cook and stir until smooth. Add cheese; stir and mix well. Serve alongside quiches.

Filled Tomato Baskets

Ingredients:

4 tomatoes
1 cup cooked roast, ground
1/2 cup salad dressing
1/2 cup chopped celery
1/4 cup chopped green pepper
1 Tbsp. minced onion or chives
salt and pepper to taste

This makes a pleasing and colorful luncheon entree.

Slice tops off tomatoes and hollow out, saving pulp. You may carve or scallop the edges of tomatoes, similar to the way you would prepare a watermelon basket, if desired.

This filling also is an excellent and hearty sandwich filling.

Mix remaining ingredients well. Fill tomato baskets with meat mixture. Serve on a bed of greens.

Use the saved tomato pulp in stew, vegetable salad, or spaghetti sauce.

Fresh green pepper halves may also be used as the baskets.

Pheasant in Sour Cream Gravy

Ingredients:
- 1 pheasant
- 1/4 cup butter
- 1/4 cup minced onion
- 1/2 tsp. garlic powder
- 1 1/2 cups sour cream
- 1 cup chicken broth or bouillon
- 1 Tbsp. Worcestershire sauce
- salt and pepper to taste

Cut pheasant into serving pieces and brown in butter. Arrange browned pieces in a baking dish.

Mix remaining ingredients together and pour over pheasant. Cover tightly. Bake in 325 degree oven until tender. This will take approximately one hour, longer if bird is mature.

Rabbit can be substituted for pheasant in this or any recipe.

Dairy products, such as butter, sour cream and cheese are naturals for cooking and flavoring any game meat. Their goodness enhances the delicate flavor more so than do onions and garlic.

The outer end of the breastbone of a young bird is quite flexible. An older bird has a more rigid breastbone.

Aging small game for 24-48 hours at a temperature just above freezing is sufficient.

Pheasant in Casserole

Ingredients:

    6 pheasant breasts
    1/4 cup butter.
    1 cup chopped onions
    1 cup chopped green peppers
    2 cups long-grain rice
    6 cups chicken broth
    1/4 tsp. crushed saffron
    2 bay leaves
    salt and pepper to taste
    1 1/2 cups frozen peas, thawed

Meats, cooked or raw, keep better when stored in glass containers.

In a large fry pan brown pheasant breasts in butter. When brown, remove pheasant pieces to a platter.

In same pan, saute onions and peppers until tender. Add rice, broth, saffron, bay leaves, salt and pepper to the vegetables. Bring to a boil.

Pour vegetable mixture into three-quart baking dish. Arrange pheasant pieces on top. Cover with foil and bake in 350 degree oven for one hour.

Lift foil and arrange thawed peas around edge. Re-cover and continue baking for another 15 minutes.

Curried Pheasant

A hunter's pride is a cook's challenge.

The sauce from this recipe also perks up left over cooked chicken and turkey. To use on leftovers, simmers sauce ingredients 15 minutes. Then add meat and continue to simmer for another ten minutes. Serve over rice.

Ingredients:
2 pheasants
1/2 cup minced onions
1/2 tsp. garlic salt
2 Tbsps. soy sauce
2 tsps. chili powder
1 tsp. tumeric
1 tsp. powdered ginger
1/2 cup olive oil
2 cups water.
rice

Remove meat from bones of two pheasants and cut into bite-sized chunks. Place meat in large saucepan and add remaining ingredients.

Simmer until pheasant is tender. Serve over rice.

Roast Duck with Apple-Sausage Stuffing

Ingredients:

1 duck
1/2 pound bulk, pork sausage
1/2 cup minced onions
1 quart dry bread crumbs
3/4 cup diced, unpeeled apple
1/2 cup chopped celery
1/4 tsp. pepper
1 tsp. dried sage
1 tsp. thyme
1 tsp. poultry seasoning
chicken bouillon (or water)

A one-pound loaf of bread makes two quarts of crumbs for stuffing.

Duck:
Soak duck in salt water overnight in refrigerator. Drain and stuff with recipe below. Bake in 350 degree oven until tender, approximately 2 1/2 hours.

Stuffing:
In large fry pan, brown sausage. Drain off all but about 1/2 cup of drippings.

Add minced onions and cook until onions are soft and tender. Transfer sausage, drippings and onions to large bowl; stir in bread crumbs, apple, celery, pepper, sage, thyme, and poultry seasoning.

Add chicken bouillon or water to moisten to desired consistency. Stuff into duck and bake as instructed above.

Paraffin and water remove down and small feathers from ducks and geese. First remove all of the feathers that you can, then try this:

For six medium birds, use 3 blocks of paraffin and 6 quarts of hot water in a deep and narrow kettle. Bring water to a boil.

Dip fowl in water, one at a time so that a coat of wax covers all feathers. Cool until wax hardens. Scrape away wax and feathers with knife.

Roast Duck, Glazed

This is elegant arranged on a serving platter with mounds of mashed, candied sweet potatoes placed around the sliced duck.

Young ducks are also good split in half and broiled. Brush often with melted butter. They also make a change-of-pace entree for an outdoor cookout when broiled over charcoals.

Ingredients:
    1 duck
    3/4 cup gin
    1 Tbsp. grated ginger root
    3/4 cup apricot-pineapple jam
    1 Tbsp. lemon juice
    1/4 cup butter

Marinate duck and refrigerate overnight in a mixture of gin and grated ginger root.

Take duck from marinade. Cover and roast in a 325 degree oven until tender (about two hours).

In saucepan, mix together jam, lemon juice and butter. Cook over low heat for five minutes.

Spread jam mixture over and inside duck. Return duck to oven and roast uncovered for 15 minutes longer. Cool slightly, slice meat from bones and arrange in center of a serving platter.

Smoked Wild Turkey

Ingredients:
- **1 wild turkey**
- **1 cup canning salt**
- **1 cup Tenderquick**
- **8 Tbsps. liquid smoke**
- **1 gallon water**
- **1 medium onion, chopped**
- **1/2 cup chopped celery and leaves**
- **2 Tbsps. pickling spices**

Combine canning salt, Tenderquick, liquid smoke, and water. Marinate wild turkey in this mixture in a deep, plastic container for four days in the refrigerator.

Remove turkey from marinade; combine onion, celery, and pickling spice. Stuff the bird with this combination.

Bake in a covered pan, breast side down (yes, this is unconventional, but it works) at 350 degrees for one hour. Reduce heat to 325 degrees and continue baking until done (about 20 minutes per pound), adding water to pan if needed. When the leg and thigh pull away easily from the cooked turkey, the meat is done.

Barbecue Meat

Meat prepared this way makes great barbecue, but it is also good used in a favorite mincemeat recipe.

Ingredients:
9 lbs. tough meat
cloves
cinnamon sticks

Clean and wash tough parts of meat; I often use meat found on lower legs. Boil hard for ten minutes in clear water. Drain and rinse meat. Boil again in clean water to which several whole cloves and cinnamon sticks have been added. When meat is done (it won't be tender yet) drain and cool. Grind the meat.

This is good used several ways, especially as a barbecue-flavored filling in deep fried sandwiches, or in a favorite mincemeat recipe.

BARBECUE MIXTURE
In large kettle add:
9 cups ground barbecue meat (see above)
2 lbs. dairy butter
6 cups barbecue sauce
4 cups tomato sauce
salt and pepper to taste

This is exceptionally good in deep-fried sandwiches.

Simmer 45 minutes. Cool and package for freezer. Can be used in deep-fried barbecued sandwiches (on next page), in other sandwiches, or any way you desire.

Dough for Deep-Fried Sandwiches

Ingredients:

- 1 pkg. dry yeast
- 3 cups warm water
- 1 tsp. salt
- 2 Tbsps. sugar
- 1/4 cup vegetable oil
- 3 cups flour
- shredded, seasoned meat

Dissolve yeast in warm water. Add salt, sugar, vegetable oil and flour; beat well:

Add more flour, one cup at a time until dough is no longer sticky. Knead five minutes. Let rise until doubled. Punch down. Pinch off egg-sized pieces of dough and flatten with hand. Place one tablespoon of meat mixture in center of dough. Form dough around filling and pinch closed. Let rise on floured surface until doubled. Deep fry in hot oil.

Serve with "Bacon Cheese Sauce" and top with chopped green pepper and onions.

I often use the barbecue mixture on the previous page for these wonderful sandwiches, but any seasoned meat could be used.

These are great prepared ahead and frozen. You may freeze them either before they are fried or after.

BACON CHEESE SAUCE

1/2 cup diced, raw bacon
1/2 cup flour
salt and pepper
milk
1 cup grated cheddar

Fry bacon until crisp. Add flour and seasonings. Cook several minutes, but do not brown. Add milk until sauce reaches desired thickness, then add cheese. Cook until melted.

Sliced Sausage Quiche

Ingredients:

1 9-inch pastry shell, unbaked
Cased sausage
1 cup shredded swiss cheese
1 cup shredded cheddar cheese
1 cup sliced mushrooms
1 Tbsp. minced onion
3 beaten eggs
1 1/2 cups half-and-half
salt and pepper to taste

Mike Jr., who makes all our sausages, describes this dish as "a dandy." It makes a wonderful entree for any meal of the day, as well as delicious hors d'oeuvres, served either hot or cold.

Another good way to use cased sausage is to place chunks of sausage in beer in a crock pot. Let pot simmer all day for a delicious treat.

Any cased sausage can be boiled for 15 minutes, then cooled before using. This seems to improve the flavor and boils out much of the fat which is sometimes added.

Prepare a 9-inch shell using a single-crust pastry recipe, pastry sticks or the quiche crust recipe on page 42. Line the pie pan with the dough, but do not bake yet.

Arrange thinly sliced and quartered pieces of any cased sauage in the bottom of the pastry shell. Of course, I use sausage made from gourmet game meat (recipes p. 71-75), and I particularly like this recipe made with summer sausage. Over the top sprinkle cheeses and mushrooms.

Blend together minced onion, eggs, half-and-half, salt and pepper. Ladle over cheese layer.

Bake in 375 degree oven for 45 minutes or until almost set in center. Let cool ten minutes before cutting and serving.

Jerky & Sausage

An Introduction to Jerky

Jerky, as it is called today, was the result of necessity. The American Indian discovered that drying meat was a way to preserve it during time of abundance for winter use and for those times when game was scarce. Learning from the Indians, pioneers took up the practice of making jerky, and dried meat was often carried in saddlebags and in wagons.

Jerky making has evolved from hanging strips of meat to dry in the sun on wooden racks to modern methods such as drying in the oven.

Many people enjoy jerky and sausages made from game meat. Since I prefer to think of game as Gourmet Meat--fit for the finest, most elegant recipes–I haven't developed personal recipes for jerky and sausage.

But many requests have been made for jerky and sausage recipes, so I went to the noted Dr. R.A. Field of the Extension Service at the University of Wyoming in Laramie. Permission has been given to use his material in this book. It is the result of many years' research.

Many thanks to Dr. Field and the UW Extension Service for sharing this useful information, on pages 56-63.

Making jerky is simple; all that is needed is a sharp knife, meat and seasonings. Use lean meat such as round steak, flank or brisket. The meat used should be trimmed of all fat and connecting tissue, then cut into strips one-half inch thick, one inch wide and as long as desired. Always cut with the grain of the meat.

Curing times vary, but always cure at refrigerated temperatures. Follow the curing times stated in recipes.

Use a thermometer to keep the drying or smoking temperature in the smokehouse or oven at 120 degrees or below. If an oven is used, line the sides and bottom with foil to catch drippings. Leave the oven door open a bit, about to the first or second stop. This allows the moisture to escape and lowers the oven temperature.

Use any hardwood for smoking. Do not use pine, fir or conifers. Remove the jerky from the smokehouse or oven before it gets too hard for your taste. Five pounds of fresh meat will make two pounds of finished jerky.

Jerky can be frozen or stored in jars or plastic bags. The color of the finished jerky can range from brown to black. Color variations depend upon the recipe used and the age and species of the animal. Meat which has been frozen and thawed can be used for making jerky. In fact, freezing meat for a month before making jerky ensures that it will be free of live parasites which are sometimes found in game meat. Meat can also be more easily cut into strips when it is a little frozen.

Simple
Dry Cured Jerky

Ingredients:

    5 lbs. meat, cut in jerky strips
    4 1/2 Tbsps. salt
    1 tsp. ground pepper
    2 Tbsps. sugar

Cut meat into thin, long, narrow jerky strips.

Spread meat out and sprinkle with salt, pepper, and sugar. Place meat into a container and refrigerate for 24 hours.

Spread strips of marinated meat on oven rack in top half of oven. Leave oven door open to first or second stop. Heat oven at 120 degrees for 48 hours or until desired dryness is reached. Use oven thermometer to make sure that oven gets no hotter than 120 degrees. Higher temperatures result in hard, brittle jerky that crumbles when eaten.

Pickle Cured Jerky

Ingredients:

>**5 lbs. fresh or frozen meat, cut into jerky strips**
>**1 gallon water**
>**3/4 cup salt**
>**1/2 cup sugar**
>**2 Tbsps. ground pepper**

Cut meat into 1/2-inch by one-inch strips.

Combine water, salt, sugar and pepper to make a marinade. Stir until salt and sugar dissolve. Other spices which may be added to marinade, according to your taste, are ten bay leaves, one teaspoon cloves, or one teaspoon sage.

Put meat strips in marinade and refrigerate overnight. Pour off marinade and let meat soak in cold tap water for one hour.

Hang strips of meat in smokehouse at 80 to 120 degrees for 48 hours, or until jerky is of desired texture. Meat may also be dried in oven as described on preceding page, but if oven is used smoke-flavor will be lacking in jerky.

Hot Pickle Cured Jerky

Ingredients:
    5 lbs. meat in jerky strips
    3/4 cup plus 4 1/2 Tbsps. salt, divided
    2 Tbsps. plus 1 tsp. pepper, divided
    1/2 cup plus 2 Tbsps. sugar, divided
    1 gallon water

This jerky may also be smoked using the smokehouse method. Hang strips of meat in smokehouse at 80 to 120 degrees for 48 hours, or until jerky reaches desired texture.

Combine the 4 1/2 tablespoons salt, the one teaspoon ground pepper and the two tablespoons sugar. Pound seasoning mixture into both sides of the jerky strips. Additional spices and liquid smoke can be added and pounded in.

Prepare a brine of one gallon water, the remaining 3/4 cup salt, the 1/2 cup sugar and the two tablespoons black pepper and heat it to a boil in a large kettle.

Immerse fresh meat strips, a few at a time, in boiling brine until they turn gray, one or two minutes. Remove meat from brine and oven dry or smoke.

Use an oven thermometer to make sure that oven gets no hotter than 120 degrees. Higher temperatures will result in hard, brittle jerky that crumbles when eaten.

Spread strips of marinated meat on oven rack in top half of oven. Leave oven door open to first or second stop. Heat oven at 120 degrees for 48 hours or until desired dryness is reached.

Marinated Jerky

Ingredients:

5 lbs. meat, cut into jerky strips
1 cup soy sauce
3 cups water
2 tsp. pepper
1 tsp. ground ginger

Start with five pounds of meat cut into jerky strips, 1/4-inch by one-inch by length desired.

Cover meat with marinade of soy sauce, salt, pepper, ginger, and water. Refrigerate for 12 hours.

Hang marinated strips of meat in smoke house at 170-190 degrees for 30 minutes. Then lower heat to 120 degrees and continue to heat until jerky is of desried hardness.

Or spread strips of marinated meat on oven rack in top half of oven. Leave oven door open to first or second stop. Heat at 120 degrees for 48 hours or until desired dryness is reached. Use oven thermometer to make sure oven gets no hotter than 120 degrees. Higher temperatures result in hard, brittle jerky that crumbles when eaten.

Ground Meat Jerky

Ingredients:
- 5 lbs. meat chunks
- 3 Tbsps. salt
- 1 Tbsp. pepper
- 2 Tbsp. sugar
- 5 Tbsp. Worcestershire Sauce

Sprinkle meat with salt, pepper, sugar, and Worcestershire.

Grind meat in meat grinder and divide it into four or five portions.

Place each portion of meat on a piece of freezer paper and flatten until it is one-inch thick. Cover meat with another piece of freezer paper. Use rolling pin to flatten meat further until it is about 1/4-inch thick.

Peel off top paper. Place a cake cooling rack or screen upside-down over meat. Then flip both rack and meat over, reversing it. Then peel off remaining sheet of paper.

Oven dry large patties at 120 degrees for 48 hours, leaving oven door slightly ajar. Or smoke in a smokehouse at 80 to 120 degrees for 48 hours until the desired dryness is reached.

Slice large patties into thin strips.

Jerky from Dry Cured Meat

Ingredients:

      10 lbs. meat, pieces 4-5 inches thick
      1 cup salt
      1/2 cup sugar
      2 tsps. saltpeter

If you have less or more than ten pounds of meat, adjust above formula to fit size of cut to be cured. Mix salt, sugar and saltpeter thoroughly. Rub surface of meat with one-third of mixture and let meat cure in refrigerator for three days.

Apply one-third of salt mixture three days later and remaining one-third on the seventh day from the time the meat was first placed in cure.

For meat over two-inches thick, cure one and one-half days per pound of meat. Cure cuts under two inches thick, seven days per inch of thickness.

After curing is complete, slice meat into one-half inch strips with the grain. Soak meat strips in cold tap water for one hour. Place in oven or smokehouse at 120 degrees for 48 hours or until desired dryness is reached.

Hunter's Jerky

Ingredients:
meat, cut in jerky strips
canning salt
liquid smoke
water

Cut meat into one-half inch slices

Prepare a brine of one part canning salt to eight parts water and bring it to a boil in a large kettle. Use kettle large enough to hold meat without crowding; water should cover meat well. Boil meat strips a few at a time for three minutes.

Dry in 120 degree oven, with door open one stop, for 48 hours or until desired dryness is reached.

Dip dried meat strips in a mixture of one-half liquid smoke and one-half water. Hang on a rack or string in open air to finish drying.

Gourmet Jerky

Ingredients:
> **1 lb. meat, cut into jerky strips**
> **1 tsp. salt**
> **1/2 tsp. pepper**
> **1/2 tsp. onion powder**
> **1/2 tsp. Worcestershire sauce**
> **2 drops bottled hot pepper sauce**

Start with one pound of meat cut with the grain into thin, long narrow strips.

Combine salt, pepper, onion powder, Worcestershire sauce and pepper sauce. Stir together in a medium-sized bowl with small amount of water until dissolved. Add meat and just enough water to cover it. Make sure meat stays submerged. Cover and refrigerate overnight.

To cook:
Drain meat and pat dry with paper towels. Lay strips on oven rack. Place foil on bottom of oven to catch drips. Set oven temperature to 150 degrees. Leave oven door slightly ajar. Drying time is from three to six hours. Check often after three hours. When it is done, it will be dark, dry and will crack sharply but will not break when bent.

Sausage Basics

Ingredients used in making the sausages in this cookbook are available in super-markets and locker plants in most areas. These recipes can be used for any game meat which has been trimmed of all fat. Any lean meat from any part of the carcass can be used for sausage. Most often, meat from the back and hind legs is used for roasts and steaks, and boneless, fat-free lean meat from other areas of the carcass is used for sausage.

It is recommended that sausage meat be removed from the carcass as soon as possible (the day after the kill is best) to prevent unnecessary bacterial growth. Meat which has been frozen and thawed can also be used.

Regardless of whether fresh or frozen meat is used, speed in sausage making is a must to prevent bacterial growth. The meat used for sausage must be free of dirt, hair, and blood-shot parts and should be trimmed of all fat. The meat should be chilled to 30 degrees Fahrenheit and made into sausage or frozen immediately.

Homemade sausages are popular among big game hunters who find that properly-handled game, when made into sausages, is palatable and highly nutritious. Also, one can spice the sausage to meet individual preferences.

Sausage Cures

A variety of prepackaged cures can be purchased at a meat processing or sausage making plant. Always follow the manufacturers directions when using a cure. Because chemicals contained in cures are potent, carefully measure ingredients when adding cure.

A cure which contains sodium nitrite will give a red color to the sausage after heating. Sausages which do not contain nitrite or nitrate cure will be brown, not red after processing.

Complete cures such as Tenderquick can also be used. Complete cures should be used in place of the total amount of salt, sugar, and cure called for in the sausage recipe. For example, if a red-colored cooked salami is desired, one cup salt, one-half cup sugar, and one teaspoon cure should be deleted from the recipe and an equivalent amount of Tenderquick added.

A meat thermometer is a must to check internal temperatures of cooked sausages such as thuringer, Polish sausage, bockwurst, liver sausage, and cooked salami.

Homemade Sausage Equipment

Stuffing sausages is easy if one has access to a sausage stuffer. If not, try making your own. One suggestion for larger casings is using a piece of plastic or stainless steel pipe and a ball bat sawed off so that it will just fit into the pipe. After the sausage is tamped into the pipe to remove the air, a casing just larger in diameter than the pipe is placed on one end, and the filled pipe is forced down over the bat. The bat pushes the sausage neatly into the casing.

Other sizes of stuffers can be homemade with plastic pipe, using a wooden dowel which fits tightly into the pipe as the plunger.

Remember that any old refrigerator must be stored carefully so that it is not a temptation for small children to climb into. Padlocking it closed with a chain through the handle helps eliminate worry.

Any plastic parts in the refrigerator which might melt should be removed.

An old refrigerator makes an excellent smokehouse, especially for jerky and sausage making. Cut a vent in the top and drill a hole in the side for an electric cord. In the bottom, set an electric hot plate with variable heat settings. An iron container filled with twigs, shavings or sawdust is placed on the hotplate.

Hang the jerky or sausages in the top of the refrigerator with string or lay it on stainless steel racks. Protect the wood from the meat drippings with a metal or foil baffle above the hotplate and under the meat. This prevents the wood from catching fire and helps eliminate smoke caused by drippings contacting the hotplate.

Sausage Casings

Pork casings, fresh or preserved in salt, along with beef, sheep, and artificial casings are available at most locker or meat processing plants where sausage is made. Casings need not be used if the game sausage is to be made into patties and fried.

All casings preserved in salt must be soaked in water for thirty minutes before use. Flush each casing by putting the end of the casing over the cold water tap and running cold water through it.

Some artificial casings need to be soaked in hot water (100 degrees) at least 30 minutes before using and then punctured with a knife point before stuffing. The purpose of puncturing the casing is to eliminate air and fat pockets in the finished sausage.

Sausage made in loaf pans needs the addition of a binder to prevent separation. To bind, bread crumbs or soy protein concentrate should be added in a proportion of five to ten percent binder to meat.

Equivalents

Some recipes, especially jerky or sausage recipes, call for seasonings by weight rather than measure. This equivalent chart, courtesy of the University of Wyoming Extension Service, will help you convert the weights if you do not have a scale.

Canning and Pickling Salt:
10.5 oz. (298 grams) = 1 cup
8.0 oz. (227 grams) = 3/4 cup
3.0 oz. (85 grams) = 4 1/2 level Tbsps.

Sugar:
5.0 oz. (141 grams) = 2/3 cup
3.5 oz. (100 grams) = 1/2 cup
1.0 oz. (28 grams) = 2 level Tbsps.

Ground Spices:
0.5 oz. (14.3 grams) = 2 level Tbsps.
0.08 oz. (2.4 grams) = 1 level tsp.

Saltpeter
0.3 oz. (8.5 grams) = 2 level tsps.

Fresh Sausage

Ingredients:

15 lbs. lean meat
10 lbs. pork or beef fat
3/4 cup canning salt
6 Tbsps. ground black pepper
5 Tbsps. rubbed sage

Grind meat and fat through coarse plate of meat grinder. Sprinkle seasonings over meat and hand mix.

Grind again through 3/16-inch grinder plate. For more highly seasoned sausage, add more pepper and one tablespoon each of ginger, nutmeg and mace.

Wrap in packages to freeze and use as fresh sausage.

Most people prefer to use pork fat in sausage. However, it is not always readily available and beef fat can also be used.

Fresh sausage should be frozen if it is going to be kept for more than four or five days in the refrigerator.

Liver Sausage

Ingredients:
- **9 lbs. liver**
- **5 lbs. lean meat**
- **4 lbs. pork fat**
- **1 lb. fresh onions**
- **3 1/2 cups plus 2 Tbsps** (0.6 lbs) **nonfat dry milk**
- **4 Tbsps. ground white pepper**
- **7 Tbsps. salt**

Fry liver until half cooked. Grind meat, liver and fat through coarse plate of meat grinder. Chop onions and add them, along with milk and pepper, to meat, hand mix.

Grind again; this time through 1/8-inch grinder plate. Mix again and stuff meat into casings which are two to three inches in diameter.

This liver sausage can also be cooked in a smokehouse at 185 degree Fahrenheit until internal temperature reaches 152 degrees. It should then be cooled and rinsed as described at right.

Cook in 170 degree water until internal temperature reaches 152 degrees Fahrenheit. Immediately place sausages in cold water until internal temperature is 100 degrees. Rinse in hot water to remove any grease. Allow to dry one to two hours at room temperature, then refrigerate.

Fresh Thuringer

Ingredients:

- 20 lbs. lean meat
- 5 lbs. pork fat
- 4 Tbsps. sugar
- 1 quart cold water
- 3/4 cup canning salt
- 3/4 cup ground white pepper
- 5 tsps. powdered mustard
- 2 tsps. cure (optional)

Liquid smoke (about 1 oz.), 1/2 oz. of cure, or both are sometimes added to thuringer.

Grind meat and fat through coarse grinder plate. Sprinkle sugar, salt, pepper and mustard over meat and hand mix.

Grind again through 3/16-inch plate while adding water, and then regrind through 1/8-inch plate.

Stuff meat into pork casings and twist casing into links.

Cook in 170 degree water or in smoke-house until internal sausage temperature is 152 degrees. Then immerse sausage into cold water until internal temperature lowers to 100 degrees.

Thuringer is allowed to stand at room temperature for one to two hours, then can be kept in the refrigerator for a few days or frozen. Or the sausage can be served hot, right from the 170 degree water or smokehouse.

Polish Sausage

Polish sausage is
sometimes made
with cured meat.
Or 1/2 ounce of cure
can be added to give
the sausages
the characteristic
red color.
See page 65.

Ingredients:

> 19 lbs. meat
> 6 lbs. pork or beef fat
> 4 1/2 cups (3/4 lb.) nonfat dry milk
> 1 cup salt
> 1/2 cup sugar
> 1 quart cold water
> 4 Tbsps. ground black pepper
> 3 Tbsps. coriander
> 5 Tbsps. garlic powder
> 2 tsps. cure (optional)

Grind meat and fat through coarse plate of meat grinder. Season by sprinkling remaining ingredients, except water, over meat and mixing by hand. Grind the meat through 1/4-inch plate while adding water; then regrind through 1/8-inch plate.

Stuff meat into pork casings.

Place sausages in smokehouse and heat at 185 degrees Fahrenheit until smoked color is obtained and sausages reach an internal temperature of 152 degrees. Immediately place sausage in cold water until internal temperature is lowered to 100 degrees. Rinse sausage with hot water to remove any grease. Allow to dry at room temperature for one to two hours. Move to refrigerator or freezer.

Cooked Salami

Ingredients:

- **19 lbs. lean meat**
- **6 lbs. pork or beef fat**
- **1 cup salt**
- **1/2 cup sugar**
- **1 quart cold water**
- **5 1/4 cups nonfat dry milk**
- **6 Tbsps. ground black pepper**
- **3 Tbsps. garlic powder**
- **3 Tbsps. coriander seed**
- **4 tsps. ground mace**
- **4 tsps. ground cardamom**
- **2 tsps. cure (optional)**

Some people like to use whole pepper in sausages, especially salami. If using whole pepper, do not add it until the meat is ground for the last time.

Grind meat and fat through coarse plate on meat grinder. Season by sprinkling remaining ingredients, except water, over meat and hand mixing. Next, grind meat through 1/4-inch plate while adding water; then regrind through 1/8-inch plate. Stuff seasoned meat into casings two to three inches in diameter.

Place in smokehouse and heat to 185 degrees Fahrenheit until internal temperature reaches 152 degrees. Move to cold water bath until internal temperature lowers to 100 degrees. Rinse with hot water to remove grease and hang sausages at room temperature for two to three hours before refrigeration. Salami should be cooled overnight in refrigerator before cutting or freezing.

If a smokehouse is unavailable, the salami may be roasted in a 185 degree oven with the door ajar. To add the smoked flavor, 1/4 cup of liquid smoke can be added.

Bockwurst

Ingredients:

- 19 lbs. meat
- 6 lbs. pork or beef fat
- 4 1/2 nonfat dry milk
- 3/4 cup salt
- 2 quarts cold water
- 3 eggs
- 2 Tbsps. sugar
- 5 Tbsps. onion powder
- 4 Tbsps. ground white pepper
- 1 Tbsp. ground mace
- 1 Tbsp. ground ginger

Grind meat and fat through coarse plate of meat grinder. Season by sprinkling remaining ingredients, except water, over meat and mixing by hand.

Grind through 1/4-inch plate while adding water. Regrind through 1/8-inch plate. Stuff seasoned meat into pork casings.

Cook in water at 170 degrees until internal temperature of sausage reaches 152 degrees Fahrenheit. Immediately place sausage in cold water until internal temperature lowers to 100 degrees.

Rinse sausage in hot water to remove any grease. Allow to dry for one or two hours at room temperature. Move to a refrigerator or freezer.

Another good way to eat this sausage is to cook it fresh, before it is cooked in the 170 degree water.

This sausage can also be placed in a smokehouse at 185 degrees until internal temperature reaches 152 degrees.

Summer Sausage

Ingredients:

  21 lbs. lean meat
  4 lbs. beef fat
  6 cups water
  5 1/4 cups nonfat dry milk
  1/2 cup sugar
  1 cup plus 2 Tbsps. salt
  1/2 cup mustard seed
  6 Tbsps. pepper
  2 1/2 Tbsps. liquid smoke
  2 Tbsps cure (see p. 65)
  **1 Tbsp plus 1 tsp. sodium
    erythorbate**

Sodium erythorbate is carried by locker plants or butchers.

Grind meat and fat through 1/2-inch plate on meat grinder. Dissolve liquid smoke, cure, and sodium erythorbate in the six cups of water. Then combine all ingredients and mix well by hand.

Stuff into casings. Cook in smokehouse at 185 degrees until internal temperature reaches 152 degrees.

Place in cold water until internal temperature is lowered to 90 degrees. Allow to hang at room temperature for two to three hours. Then refrigerate or freeze.

Hermie's Canned Trout

Ingredients:
  trout
  1 gallon cold water
  1 cup canning salt
  Plus additional ingredients from
      variation of your choice.
Before you start, estimate number of pint jars you will need and check recipe to assure that you have enough ingredients for number of jars you'll be filling.

Make brine of the gallon of cold water and canning salt. Soak fish in brine for one to two hours.

Drain fish well and cut into chunks. Pack chunks into hot, sterilized pint jars, leaving one-half inch of space at top.

To top of each jar, add ingredients from variation which you select from those listed on these pages..

After ingredients are added to top of jar, place lids on jars, screwing band tight. Cook in pressure cooker for 90 minutes at ten pounds of pressure.

VARIATION #1
Add to the top of each jar:
  2 Tbsps. canned tomato soup

To prepare the trout for canning, clean the fish and remove the heads and tails. The bones remain in the fish and will become soft, as in canned salmon.

This is delicious cold from the jar. Or try it creamed and served with a side dish of spinach noodles.

See next page for more variations on this same canning recipe.

Variations on Hermie's Trout

VARIATION #2
Add to the top of each jar:
> 1 Tbsps. prepared mustard
> 1 Tbsp. oil

VARIATION #3
Add to top of each jar:
> 1 1/2 tsps. salt
> 1 tsp. vinegar
> 1 Tbsp. oil

VARIATION #4
Add to top of each jar:
> 1 tsp. salt
> 1 Tbsp oil
> 1 Tbsp. catsup

VARIATION #5
Add to top of each jar:
> 2 1/4 tsps. catsup
> 2 tsps. oil
> 2 1/4 tsps. vinegar
> 1/2 tsp. salt

This delicacy is a compliment-getter when served cold on a platter of shredded greens, garnished with lemon wedges and stuffed olives.

Try Hermie's Trout as an appetizer. Serve it cold on a tray with Swiss cheese strips and sweet pickle chunks alongside.

Vegetables & Salads

Equivalents

1 cup uncooked rice = 3 1/2 cups cooked
1 cup uncooked macaroni = 2 cups cooked
1 cup uncooked noodles = 1 3/4 cups cooked
1/2 pound uncooked spaghetii = 4 cups cooked
1 cup uncooked barley = 4 cups cooked
1 medium clove garlic = 1/8 tsp. garlic powder
1 lemon, squeezed = 2 1/2-3 1/2 Tbsps. juice

Wines to Make Meals Festive

Red wines with red meat = Serve cold
Red wines with fowl = Serve at room temperature
White wines with white meat = Serve cold
White wines with fish = Serve cool

Vegetables & Salads

The following vegetable and salad recipes are favorites from my files and from those of family and friends. They have been served over the years with the Gourmet Game Meat recipes in this volume. They complement any meal, but seem to taste especially good with Gourmet Meat recipes.

With the exception of onions and garlic, all vegetables blend well when cooked with Gourmet Meat. Onions and garlic seem best when cooked separately and added to the cooked dish before serving.

Potatoes Julie

Julie makes a hobby of cooking delicious meals. This dish is one that travels nicely to gatherings, because it doesn't need to be eaten right out of the oven to be good.

Try baking this in a ten-inch square pan and cutting it into squares for serving. Add a tablespoon of sour cream to the top of each square just before serving. This recipes serves six and reheats well.

Ingredients:

3 cups grated potatoes
3/4 cup minced onions
1 cup grated Swiss cheese
5 slices crisp bacon, crumbled
2 eggs, beaten
1/4 cup bread crumbs
salt and pepper to taste

In large bowl combine eggs, crumbs, salt and pepper. Add potatoes, onions and one-half of cheese and bacon.

Pour into buttered baking dish. Sprinkle remaining cheese and bacon over top.

Bake in 350 degree oven for 30 minutes.

Potato Dumplings

Ingredients:

    4 large, unpeeled potatoes
    4 eggs, separated
    1/2 cup water
    salt and pepper to taste
    1/4 cup flour, plus more as needed
    2 cups chicken broth, plus more as needed

Potato Dumplings are good served with "Chops and Cabbage" made with the recipe on page 23.

Boil four large, unpeeled potatoes. When cooked, cool, peel and mash.

Separate egg yolks from whites. Beat egg yolks with 1/2 cup of cool water. Add salt and pepper.

Save the egg whites and add them to tomorrow morning's scrambled eggs or to another recipe.

Add egg yolk mixture to mashed potatoes and mix well. Stir in flour; start by adding 1/4 cup, then add more, a tablespoonful at a time, to make a firm dough.

Bring two cups of chicken broth to a boil in a tall saucepan. Shape dough into walnut-sized balls. Drop dough-balls, a few at a time, into boiling chicken broth. Simmer for ten minutes. Remove dumplings from broth and drain. Add more broth to saucepan as needed. Repeat until all dough is cooked.

Sweet Potato Surprise

Ingredients:

4 medium sweet potatoes
3 medium oranges
1 3-oz. pkg. cream cheese, softened
4 Tbsps. butter, softened
1/2 cup brown sugar
1/2 tsp. pumpkin pie spice
marshmallows

Boil, cool, peel and mash four sweet potatoes.

Cut oranges in half and remove pulp. Save skins. Run pulp and juice through a blender until pulp is chopped fine.

In large bowl mix together blended pulp, cream cheese, butter, brown sugar and pumpkin pie spice.

Place mixture into buttered baking dish. Bake 45 minutes at 350 degrees.

When baked, fill hollowed-out orange shells with hot sweet potatoes; place marshmallow on top. Return to oven, watching carefully until marshmallow puffs and browns. Serve immediately.

Saucy Onions

Ingredients:

    2 cups white sauce
    2 Tbsps. chicken bouillon
    1/2 cup white wine
    2/3 cup milk
    salt and pepper to taste
    1/4 cup grated parmesan cheese
    2 Tbsps. chopped parsley
    1/4 cup minced pimento
    2 cups onions, in rings
    2 Tbsps. butter

Saute onion rings in butter.

Mix together white sauce, bouillon, wine, and milk. Heat to boiling, stirring constantly. Add salt and pepper to taste. Stir in cheese and pimento. Add parsley.

Layer onions in baking dish. Pour white sauce mixture over onions.

Bake in 375 degree oven for 25 minutes.

WHITE SAUCE

4 T. butter
4 T. flour
2 cups milk
1/2 t. dry mustard
salt & pepper to taste

Melt butter over low heat; add and blend flour and dry mustard. Cook in saucepan for four minutes. Stir in milk.

Stir constantly to avoid lumping. Cook until thickened.

If sauce lumps, strain it through wire mesh strainer.

Onions a la Dee

Canned evaporated milk may be used as a substitute for half-and-half in this recipe and in most others.

Dee often serves this tasty and unusual dish with a Gourmet Game roast.

Ingredients:
3 onions
1/4 cup butter
3 eggs
1/4 cup half-and-half
1/4 tsp. nutmeg
1/2 cup cooked, crumbled bacon
salt and pepper to taste

Peel onions and soak for 45 minutes in cold, salt water. Drain and slice.

Saute onions in butter until tender. Do not brown. While onions are cooking, beat three eggs.

Add to eggs: half-and-half, nutmeg, salt and pepper. Mix.

Arrange onions in a 1-1/2 quart baking dish. Spread cooked, crumbled bacon over top. Over this, pour egg mixture.

Bake in 350 degree oven until knife inserted into center comes out clean, approximately 45 minutes. Let set ten minutes before serving.

Celery/Mushroom Treat

Ingredients:

2 Tbsps. butter
2 cups diced celery
2 cups sliced mushrooms
1/2 tsp. grated ginger root (or 1/4
        tsp. powdered ginger)
1 Tbsp. soy sauce
1 Tbsp. brown sugar
1/4 cup chopped pimento

Melt butter in a fry pan. Add celery and mushrooms and cook until tender.

Blend in ginger, soy sauce, brown sugar and pimento.

Pour into serving dish and enjoy.

Ginger is a true spice, the root of a plant that grows in Southeast Asia, Cuba, Africa and Jamaica. Ginger was one of the first Oriental spices known in Europe, but was used in medicine long before it was used in food.

Use this versatile spice in cookies, gingerbread, pumpkin pies, carrots, fruit, sweet potatoes, meringues, marinades and Oriental cooking.

Many cooks prefer to freshly grate ginger, rather than use powdered ginger because of the enhanced subtle flavor.

Cabbage in Potato Sauce

Sauerkraut can be used in place of the cabbage and is also delicious in this recipe.

This is an old Polish recipe given to me by my mother-in-law. She brought it to the U.S. when she came from Poland in 1910. It is a favorite of my family and is especially complementary to game bird recipes.

Ingredients:
1 head cabbage, medium-sized
1 large potato
2 cups water, divided
3 strips bacon
salt and pepper to taste

Shred one small to medium-sized head of cabbage. Put in saucepan with 1-1/2 cups of water. Boil slowly for ten minutes or until tender.

In blender, grate potato with 1/2 cup of water.

Cut three strips of bacon into small pieces and fry.

When bacon is crisp, add potato mixture to fry pan, cooking and stirring until thickened, about five minutes. Add salt and pepper to taste.

When potato mixture is thickened, add it to the cooked, undrained cabbage. Mix well and let simmer another few minutes.

This dish reheats well. In fact, the taste seems to get even better when it is reheated.

The Best Broccoli

Ingredients:

      2 pkgs. frozen broccoli, cooked
      1 1/2 cups seasoned stuffing mix
      1 cup sour cream
      1/2 cup sliced mushrooms
      3/4 cup milk
      1/4 cup mayonnaise
      1 Tbsp. Worcestershire Sauce

In a small bowl, combine and mix: sour cream, mushrooms, milk, mayonnaise and Worcestershire Sauce.

Place half the cooked, drained broccoli in a buttered casserole. Cover with half the stuffing mix. Then ladle on half of the sauce mixture. Repeat layers of remaining broccoli, stuffing and sauce, ending with the sauce.

Bake in 350 degree oven for 40 minutes.

Broccoli Souffle

Ingredients:

> 3 Tbsps. butter
> 3 Tbsps. all-purpose flour
> 3 tsps. chicken bouillon
> 2 tsps. minced onion
> 1 1/2 tsps. dill weed
> 1/4 tsp. nutmeg
> dash cayenne pepper
> 1 cup milk
> 1 1/4 cups diced broccoli
> 1 Tbsp. lemon juice
> 4 eggs, separated

Melt butter; stir in flour, bouillon, dill, nutmeg, onion and cayenne pepper. Cook mixture until bubbly; then remove from heat. Stir in milk and cook over low heat until thickened, stirring constantly.

Remove from heat; add broccoli and lemon juice.

Beat egg yolks until thick, then add to broccoli mixture, stirring quickly. Let cool.

While broccoli mixture is cooling, beat egg whites until stiff. Fold whites gently into broccoli mixture.

Pour into a buttered 1-1/2 quart casserole. Bake in a pan of hot water in 375 degree oven for 40 minutes. Serves six.

Carrot Surprise

Ingredients:
- 1 1/2 Tbsps. cornstarch
- 2 cups milk
- 4 Tbsps. melted butter
- 1/2 tsp. salt
- 2 Tbsps. brown sugar
- 4 beaten eggs
- 3 cups cooked, mashed carrots

Combine cornstarch, milk, butter, salt and brown sugar. Add the beaten eggs and cooked, mashed carrots.

Pour mixture into a buttered baking dish. Bake one hour in 350 degree oven.

This recipe came to me by way of Texas. A friend found it in her travels.

Sweet & Sour Carrots

This recipe came to me from Betty in Salt Lake City. She keeps it in the fridge and serves it with burgers and chips.

Ingredients:
- 2 lbs. carrots
- 1 medium onion, chopped
- 1/4 cup chopped celery
- 1 medium green pepper, chopped
- 1 can tomato soup, undiluted
- 1/2 cup vinegar
- 1 Tbsp. Worcestershire Sauce
- 1 tsp. dry mustard
- 1 tsp. salt
- 3/4 cup brown sugar
- 3/4 cup salad oil

Peel and slice carrots; cook in salted water until tender. Drain and cool.

In a separate bowl, combine remaining ingredients together and mix well.

Pour sauce over carrots. Refrigerate and serve cold.

This keeps well in the refrigerator for several days.

Two Good Beet Dishes

BEETS IN SAUCE
Ingredients:

    2 cups cooked, diced beets, drained
    2 Tbsps. brown sugar
    1 Tbsp. cornstarch
    1 Tbsp. lemon juice
    1 Tbsp. butter
    1/2 cup orange juice concentrate
    3/4 cup water

Both canned beets and fresh cooked beets work nicely in these recipes.

Mix sugar and cornstarch. Stir in orange concentrate and water. Cook and stir until thick. Stir in lemon juice and butter. Add beets last and heat through.

NEW YORK BEETS
Ingredients:

    2 cups diced, cooked beets, drained
    1/2 cup sour cream
    1/2 tsp. horseradish
    salt and pepper to taste

This is a colorful dish which is excellent when served as an accompaniment to Gourmet Game roast or steak.

Mix the beats and sour cream. Add horseradish and salt and pepper.

Heat, but do not boil. Serve immediately.

Scalloped Tomatoes

Ingredients:

3 cups cooked tomatoes
3 strips bacon
2 cups soda crackers
1/2 cup water
1/4 cup green pepper, chopped
1/3 cup onions, chopped fine
1/4 tsp. pepper

A quick and easy method to have just the right amount of tomatoes when you need them is to freeze them whole.

Wash and dry whole fresh tomatoes. Freeze them on cookie sheets; then put them into plastic bags.

When ready to use, wash frozen tomatoes in warm water. This softens the skins, so they can be easily removed. Cut out the stem end, and then cook the tomatoes.

Chop bacon into small pieces and fry. Save drippings.

Layer half the tomatoes in baking dish, top with half the bacon, then add half the onions and peppers, and half the soda crackers. Repeat layering with remaining ingredients.

Mix water, bacon drippings and pepper. Pour over top.

Bake in 350 degree oven for 30 minutes.

Broiled Tomatoes

Ingredients:
- **4 fresh tomatoes**
- **1/2 cup sour cream**
- **1/4 cup mayonnaise**
- **1 Tbsp. minced onion**
- **1/8 tsp. dried dill weed**
- **1/4 tsp. salt**
- **butter**
- **salt and pepper**

Mix sour cream, mayonnaise, onion, dill and salt together and refrigerate for two hours.

Cut tomatoes in half. Sprinkle with salt and pepper; dot with butter.

Broil with cut side up a few inches from heat for five minutes.

Spoon sauce over tomatoes just before serving.

Corn Bake

This makes good picnic fare, although you'll probably want to double the recipe for picnics and potlucks because it's a real favorite. It's delicious served hot or cold.

Ingredients:

- 2 cups whole kernel corn
- 1 cup crushed soda crackers
- 1/2 cup diced celery
- 1/4 cup minced onion
- 1/4 cup minced pimento
- 3/4 cup grated American cheese
- 2 eggs, beaten
- 2 Tbsps. melted butter
- 1 cup milk

Combine and mix ingredients. Place in buttered casserole.

Bake in 350 degree oven for 35 minutes.

Grits Elegant

Ingredients:

4 cups boiling water
1 cup regular grits (do not use
instant grits)
1/2 tsp. salt
1/2 cup butter
1 1/4 cup grated cheddar, divided
3 beaten eggs
1/2 cup milk

This is an old family recipe from a Southern friend. It's a real compliment-getter because it is unusual, but very good.

Pour grits into boiling water. Continue to cook over low heat, stirring constantly, until all water is absorbed. Add butter, one cup of the cheese, eggs and milk.

Place mixture in 1-1/2 quart casserole which has been greased. Sprinkle remaining 1/4 cup of cheese on top.

Bake in 350 degree oven for 30 minutes.

Sylvia's CC

This recipe came from Iowa with my sister-in-law Sylvia. She uses fresh corn when it's available.

SIMPLE CORNBREAD

*1 cup yellow cornmeal
1 cup flour
3 T. sugar
4 1/2 t. baking powder
salt to taste
1/4 cup oil
1 egg, beaten
1 1/4 cup milk*

Preheat oven to 400 degrees.

Combine dry ingredients. Add milk, oil eggs. Mix until blended.

Bake in a greased 8-by-11 inch pan for 25 minutes in a 400 degree oven.

Ingredients:
**1/2 cup butter
1 1/2 cups cream style corn
1 1/2 cups whole kernel corn
2 beaten eggs
1 cup sour cream
1 box (small) corn bread mix**

Melt butter over low heat. Add both kinds of corn, eggs, and sour cream. Mix well.

Add entire box of cornbread mix, all at once. Stir until moist. If no cornbread mix is on hand, you may use the flour, cornmeal, sugar, baking powder, and salt from the Simple Cornbread Recipe at left (do not mix in the moist ingredients listed).

Bake in greased 1-1/2 quart baking dish at 350 degrees for 45 minutes. Serves eight.

Beet Salad

Ingredients:

    2 cups diced, pickled beets,
        drained, save juice
    1 3-oz. pkg. lemon flavored gelatin
    1 cup boiling water
    1 tsp. minced onion
    2 Tbsps. lemon juice
    1 cup diced, unpeeled apple
    mayonnaise

You really need to taste this dish to appreciate its good flavor.

Dissolve gelatin in boiling water; add 3/4 cup of beet juice, lemon juice and onions. Chill until mixture begins to thicken; then fold in beets and apple.

Pour into 1-1/2 quart mold. Chill until firm. Garnish with mayonnaise.

Different Aspic

To soften gelatin, just let it stand in liquid for about five minutes.

Ingredients:
- 1 1/4 cups mixed vegetable juice
- salt to taste
- 1 pkg. unflavored gelatin
- 1/4 cup cold water
- 3/4 cups white wine
- 1 Tbsp. wine vinegar
- 1/4 cup crumbled blue cheese
- 1/2 cup minced celery
- 1 tsp. minced onions

Soften gelatin in 1/4 cup of cold water. Heat juice and salt to boiling. Add softened gelatin. Stir until gelatin dissolves. Blend in wine and vinegar. Chill.

When partially thickened, fold in blue cheese, onions and celery. Chill until firm.

Molded Mixed Vegetables

Ingredients:

    1 3-oz. pkg. lime gelatin
    1 cup boiling water
    3/4 cup white wine
    2 Tbsps. lime juice
    2 Tbsps. sugar
    2 cups mixed vegetables, cooked,
          drained and cooled
    1/2 cup celery, chopped
    1 Tbsp. onion, minced

Cook, drain and cool mixed vegetables.

Dissolve gelatin in boiling water and add wine. Then add lime juice and sugar. Mix this mixture well and chill.

When mixture begins to thicken, add mixed vegetables, celery and onion.

Pour into a mold and chill until firm.

This is excellent for a salad luncheon. Try it with Gourmet Meat salads.

A combination of peas, corn, lima beans, green peppers and red peppers is especially good, and colorful also.

Some good combinations of vegetables are packaged together and sold in the frozen foods section of most supermarkets.

For individual salad molds, I use plastic "Dixie-cup-type" ice cream containers. The half cup size is perfect for a single serving.

Two Unusual Molded Salads

The recipe for this delicious tart salad was sent from California. Its tanginess complements all of the Gourmet Meat recipes.

GRAPEFRUIT AND AVOCADO SALAD

Ingredients:

- 1 3-oz. pkg. lemon gelatin
- 1 1/2 cups boiling water.
- 1/2 cup unsweetened grapefruit juice
- 1/2 cup diced grapefruit sections
- 1/2 cup diced orange sections
- 1 1/2 cups diced avocado

Dissolve lemon gelatin in boiling water. Add grapefruit juice. Chill until mixture begins to thicken.

Add grapefruit sections, orange sections, and diced avocado. Chill until set.

MOLDED KIDNEY BEAN SALAD

Ingredients:

- 1 3-oz. pkg lemon gelatin
- 1 cup boiling water
- 1 cup cottage cheese
- 1/2 cup French dressing
- 1 Tbsp. minced onion
- 1 cup kidney beans, rinsed and drained
- 1 cup finely shredded cabbage

Dissolve gelatin in boiling water. Chill until it begins to thicken. Stir in remaining ingredients. Chill until firm.

Two Quick Fruit Salads

QUICK FRUIT SLAW

Ingredients:

3 cups finely shredded cabbage
1 cup pineapple chunks, drained
1 unpeeled apple, chopped fine
1 cup miniature marshmallows
1/2 cup chopped celery
1 cup mayonnaise

Mix together and chill.

OPAL'S QUICK ORANGE SALAD

Ingredients:

1 large container cottage cheese
1 large can crushed pineapple,
   partially drained
1 large pkg. orange flavored
   gelatin
1 cup oranges, chopped and
   drained
1 large container non-dairy frozen
   topping, softened

Opal serves this salad with Christmas dinner. It has become a tradition in her household.

Mix together cottage cheese and pineapple. Add the gelatin and stir until dissolved. Add oranges. Fold in the topping.

Chill until set.

Festive Salad

This recipe is part of the Holiday Buffet menu suggested on page 14.

Ingredients:

- 1 1/2 cups crushed pineapple
- 2 3-oz. pkgs. lemon flavored gelatin
- 2 cups ginger ale
- 1 cup jellied cranberry sauce
- 1 large container non-dairy frozen topping, softened
- 1 8-oz. pkg. cream cheese, softened
- 1/2 cup chopped nuts

Drain pineapple, save juice, adding enough water to juice to make one cup of liquid. Heat liquid to boiling; add gelatin and stir until dissolved. Let cool.

Stir in ginger ale. Chill until partially set.

Fold in pineapple and cranberry sauce.

Spread into a 9-by-9-by-2 inch dish. Chill until firm.

Blend cream cheese and topping together; spread over gelatin layer. Sprinkle nuts over top.

Cream Slaw

Ingredients:

1 gallon cabbage, cut fine
1 1/4 cups vinegar
1/2 cup water
1/2 cup sugar
1 Tbsp. butter
2 eggs
1 pint sour cream
1 tsp. flour
1 Tbsp. salt
1/2 tsp. pepper
1 Tbsp. dry mustard

When cabbage is plentiful, I keep this salad on hand in the fridge for quick summer meals. It will keep for several days when refrigerated.

Add vinegar, water, sugar, and butter to saucepan and bring to boil.

Mix together eggs, sour cream, flour, salt, pepper and mustard. Stir sour cream mixture into vinegar mixture and cook until thickened. Cool and pour over cabbage. Mix well.

Cucumber-Pineapple Salad

ANOTHER CUCUMBER SALAD

Blend:
1 cup plain yogurt
1 t. salt
1/2 t. paprika

Add:
2 medium cucumbers, peeled and sliced;
2 medium tomatoes, chopped;
1 green pepper, diced;
1 onion, sliced into rings.

Chill and serve

Ingredients:
>1 large cucumber
>1/2 cup stuffed olives, finely chopped
>2 cups crushed pineapple, drain and save juice
>1 3-oz. pkg. lime gelatin
>1/2 cup sour cream

Peel and finely chop cucumber. Add water to pineapple juice to make 1 1/4 cups of liquid. Heat water and juice to boiling. Add gelatin and stir until dissolved.

Chill until partially set.

Blend in sour cream, cucumber, olives, and pineapple.

Pour into a one quart casserole and chill until firm.

Rhubarb Salad

Ingredients:
- **2 cups rhubarb, cooked, drained**
- **2 cups pineapple juice**
- **2 cups raw apples, chopped**
- **2 3-oz. pkgs. strawberry gelatin**
- **1 cup walnuts, chopped**
- **sour cream**

Bring rhubarb and pineapple juice to boil. Remove from heat and add gelatin. Cool.

Add apples and chopped nuts.

Pour into mold and chill. Serve with sour cream.

I sometimes make this tangy salad in individual molds and place each serving on a salad plate with a bed of greens.

Hot Breads

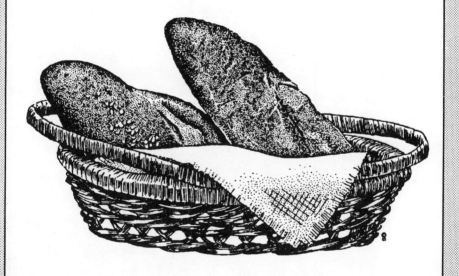

Two things only
the people anxiously desire–
bread and circuses.

Juvenal (47-138 A.D.)

Hot Breads

The aroma of hot bread has drawn many picky eaters to the table. Not many can resist the mouth-watering thoughts that the smell of hot bread brings to mind.

The hot bread recipes on the following pages have been generously shared by family and friends from their extra-special files. They've been used over and over again throughout the years, and many of them have been passed from one generation to another.

I enjoy baking and serving these breads to complement my Gourmet Meat dishes. I've noted in the sidebars some of the meats and breads which especially enhance each other.

I like Herbed Rolls with the Moist Roast recipe in the meat section. Kay's Cornmeal Buns go especially well with Mexican flavored dishes and Lithuanian Rye Bread is delicious when used to make a sandwich with summer sausage.

Use your imagination and you, too, will find your favorites to enhance Gourmet Meat meals.

Sourdough Starter

Ingredients:

2 cups warm water
1 pkg. active dried yeast (or 1 yeast cake or 1 Tbsp. dried yeast)
2 cups white flour

Put warm water into a non-metal container with a lid; a glass quart jar works nicely. Add yeast and flour.

Mix ingredients to form a smooth paste. Put lid on so that it fits loosely. Place container in a warm place for 24 hours, or longer if a more tangy flavor is desired. The sourdough starter will be full of small bubbles. It will keep in refrigerator and you may use from it, replenishing remaining starter. In the refrigerator, the low temperature will cause the bubbles to disappear and a clear liquid will rise to the top. This is normal; just stir before using.

Each time starter is used, save back one cup. Return this cup of starter to container and replace what you've used by adding a flour and water replenisher. To replenish, mix 3/4 cup flour and 1/4 cup water into a smooth paste; add it to container. Let it work in container for a day before refrigerating. Mixture will improve with time.

This recipe for sourdough was used by old timers in the days of the early West. My uncle, who came to Wyoming on one of the early cattle drives from Texas, always had this starter bubbling in his small kitchen. I remember the delicious aroma and taste of his sourdough biscuits.

While some sourdough bread purchased in stores is very strong and tangy, bread made from this starter has a more subtle flavor.

This wholesome bread is finding favor in many kitchens today, just as Gourmet Meats are, by those who appreciate good eating.

See the Sourdough Chocolate Cake on page 137 of the dessert section.

Sourdough Biscuits

Ingredients:
- **2 cups sourdough starter (p. 112)**
- **1 tsp. salt**
- **1 Tbsp. shortening**
- **1 tsp. baking soda**
- **4 cups flour**
- **warm water**

Mix together the dry ingredients and add the starter. Add enough warm water to make a soft, but not sticky, dough. Mix well and roll out on a floured surface until the dough is about one-inch thick.

Cut biscuits and place on a greased baking sheet. Bake in a 375 degree oven for 15-20 minutes.

Hearty sourdough breads don't belong entirely to the legendary past of the Old West's "Sourdoughs"–the prospectors, miners, and trappers who acquired the nickname from their bread. According to Pliny's Natural History, sourdough was in use during the days of the Pharaohs, the Roman Empire, and the Ancient Egyptians.

Sourdough Pancakes

For another good and unusual recipe, try the Sourdough Chocolate Cake in the dessert section.

Ingredients:

- **1 cup sourdough starter** (p. 112)
- **2 cups warm water**
- **2 1/2 cups flour**
- **1/4 cup warm milk**
- **1 tsp. salt**
- **1/2 tsp. baking soda**
- **2 Tbsps. vegetable oil or bacon drippings**
- **1 egg**

The night before you want to cook pancakes, put a cup of sourdough starter into a mixing bowl. Add warm water and flour. Mix well, cover with plastic wrap, and let set in a warm place overnight.

The next morning, remove one cup of pancake batter and put it back into the sourdough-starter container to replace the amount you took out. To remaining batter add milk, salt, soda, and oil or drippings. Mix well; then add egg. Mix again and let set for eight minutes. Fry pancakes on a lightly greased griddle.

Sourdough Date Loaf

Ingredients:

    1/2 cup sourdough starter (p 112)
    1 cup evaporated milk
    2 Tbsps. sugar
    1 1/2 cups flour
    1/2 cup oatmeal
    1 tsp. baking powder
    1/2 tsp. baking soda
    1/4 tsp. salt
    1 tsp. cinnamon
    2 eggs, beaten
    1 cup chopped dates
    1 cup chopped pecans

This is a delicious breakfast bread, served with butter and jam. It can also be used as a party bread, served with cream cheese.

The night before you wish to bake the date loaf, combine starter, evaporated milk, sugar, and flour. Let mixture set at room temperature overnight.

The next morning, mix oatmeal, baking powder, baking soda, salt, cinnamon, and beaten eggs. Add to sourdough batter and mix well. Then add chopped dates and pecans.

Bake in 350 degree oven for 45-50 minutes or until golden brown.

Yam Bread

Ingredients:
   3/4 cup cooked, mashed yams
   1/4 cup milk
   1/4 cup orange juice
   2 Tbsps. honey
   1/2 cup brown sugar, packed
   1/2 cup white sugar
   1/2 cup butter
   2 eggs
   1 1/4 cups flour
   1/2 tsp. baking soda
   1/2 cup raisins
   1/2 cup chopped nuts

Mix milk, yams, orange juice and honey together.

In a separate bowl, cream together butter, sugar, and eggs. Stir flour, raisins and nuts into butter mixture.

Add flour combination to the yam mixture and mix well.

Pour into greased 9-by-5-by-3 inch loaf pan. Bake in 350 degree oven for 40 minutes.

Then cover bread with foil and continue baking a few more minutes until toothpick inserted into center comes out clean.

Saffron Buns

Ingredients:

- 3/4 cup milk
- 1/8 tsp. saffron
- 1/2 cup corn oil
- 1/4 cup sugar
- 1 tsp. salt
- 1 pkg. dry yeast
- 1/4 cup warm water
- 2 eggs, beaten
- 1/2 cup dried currants
- 1 tsp. nutmeg
- 4-6 cups flour

Scald milk (see sidebar p. 120) and saffron. In a large bowl combine milk mixture, oil, sugar, and salt. Soften yeast in water until dissolved, then add to mixture in bowl.

Next add eggs, currants, nutmeg and enough flour (about 4-6 cups) to make a stiff dough. Knead for ten minutes.

Let rise until doubled, about 45 minutes.

Shape into small balls and place in greased pans. Brush tops with egg white and let rise until again doubled, about 45 minutes.

Bake in preheated 425 degree oven for 20 minutes or until done.

Frost with powder sugar frosting.

Saffron is sometimes hard to find in supermarkets, but it is generally stocked in gourmet spice and cooking shops. It is expensive, but a little goes a long way.

Because of its potency, measure it carefully and use no more than is called for. It comes in threads and is used as is.

Saffron has been used in cookery for centuries. It had early medicinal uses and was used as a perfume.

POWDERED SUGAR FROSTING

Mix together in the order listed:

1/2 cup butter
3 cups powdered sugar
2 t. vanilla
4-5 t. milk

Beat until fluffy. Spread on rolls.

Potato Rolls

*My mother served
these rolls with
Gourmet Chicken
Fried Steak (p. 16)
and Broiled
Tomatoes (p. 95)*

Ingredients:

    1 1/4 cups mashed potatoes
    1 1/2 cups butter, softened
    3 eggs
    1 1/2 tsps. salt
    1/2 cup sugar
    6 1/2 cups flour
    1 1/2 cups warm water
    1 pkg. dry yeast

Dissolve yeast in water. Add potatoes and butter; mix well.

Add eggs, salt, sugar, and two cups of flour. Mix well. Mix in remaining flour, two cups at a time, but do not knead. Put into a container which allows room for dough to rise. Cover container with tight lid. Refrigerate overnight.

Remove dough from refrigerator four hours before serving. When dough has doubled in size, roll into 1/2 inch-thickness and cut with biscuit cutter.

Let rise on greased baking sheet until double in size, about an hour.

Bake in a 425 degree oven for 15-25 minutes, until golden brown.

Herbed Rolls

Ingredients:

- 1 cup warm water
- 1 pkg. dry yeast
- 1 tsp. dried tarragon, crushed
- 1 tsp. celery seed
- 1 tsp. parsley, dried and crushed
- 2 Tbsps. sugar
- 1 tsp. salt
- 1/4 cup vegetable oil
- 3 cups flour

In large mixing bowl, combine water and yeast. When yeast has dissolved, add remaining ingredients.

Mix and knead well. Add more flour if dough is sticky. Cover and let rise until double, about 45 minutes. Punch down.

Make into dinner rolls (see sidebar). Place on greased baking sheet about 1/2-inch apart. Let rise until double, about 45 minutes.

Bake in 375 degree oven for 15 minutes.

These rolls go especially well with the roasts on page 27.

To shape a dinner roll, pinch off a piece of dough about the size of an egg. Form it in your hands until it is round and smooth.

This recipe also makes good cloverleaf rolls. Shape dough into three walnut-sized balls. Place three balls into each cup of a greased muffin tin and bake.

Kay's Cornmeal Buns

This recipe comes from a ranch wife and is a favorite of her family. She uses fresh milk which should be scalded.

Milk is scalded by heating it until tiny bubbles form around the edge of the pan, at about 180 degrees. In this age of pasteurization, scalding is no longer required, but heating the milk does help dissolve dry ingredients and liquefy butter.

Ingredients:

2 pkgs. dry yeast
1/4 cup warm water
2 cups milk, scalded
3/4 cup cornmeal
1/2 cup sugar
1/2 cup butter
2 tsps. salt
3 eggs, beaten
6 1/2 cups white flour

Dissolve dry yeast in warm water.

Scald milk (see sidebar); add cornmeal. Cook for one minute, stirring continually. Cool to luke-warm.

Add sugar, salt, eggs, butter, and flour to cornmeal mixture. Then add dissolved yeast. Make into stiff dough.

Let rise until double in size, about an hour. Punch down and let rise until doubled again, about 30-45 minutes

Pinch off dough and shape into buns, each about the size of an egg. Place on a baking sheet about 1/2-inch apart and let rise again until doubled in bulk.

Bake in 400 degree oven for 15 minutes.

These are great served with the Mexican-flavored dishes in the meat section.

Oatmeal Rolls

Ingredients:

- 1 3/4 cups boiling water
- 1 1/2 cups quick-cooking oatmeal
- 1/4 cup butter
- 1/2 cup molasses
- 6 cups flour, divided
- 1/2 cup powdered milk
- 1 1/2 tsps. salt
- 2 pkgs. dry yeast
- 2 eggs

Combine boiling water and oatmeal. Let mixture set for five minutes. Then add butter and molasses to oatmeal.

In a separate bowl, mix two cups of flour, powdered milk, salt and yeast. Add this to oatmeal mixture and beat for two minutes. Add two additional cups of flour and eggs. Beat well.

Add final two cups of flour and knead for five minutes.

Cover and let rise until double, about one hour. Punch down and make into small dough balls. Place on a greased pan with the rolls just touching. Let rise until double, about 30-45 minutes.

Bake in preheated oven at 400 degrees for 20 minutes.

Lithuanian Rye Bread

Ingredients:

2 pounds dark, rye flour (about 6 cups)

1 wine-glass vinegar (about 1/2 cup)

boiling water

2 tsps. salt

2 tsps. caraway seeds

1/2 cup sugar

1 1/4 cups warm water, divided

2 pkgs. dry yeast

flour, all-purpose white

Rye flour often comes in 2-pound boxes.

This recipe will make two small loaves or one larger round loaf. If making the round loaf, use a round pan and shape dough to the pan. If making two loaves, divide dough in half and form each loaf.

This is delicious when made into sandwiches using sausage made with recipes in this book.

Dilute vinegar with equal amount of boiling water. Stir in rye flour. Add enough boiled water to make thin paste. Add salt and caraway seeds. Let cool.

Dissolve sugar and one package of yeast in one cup of warm water. Stir yeast/sugar into rye mixture while still slightly warm. Cover with cloth and let set overnight in a warm place.

In the morning, dissolve other package of yeast in 1/4 cup of warm water. Add yeast to rye mixture. Stir in enough all-purpose white flour to make stiff dough. Stir vigorously.

Let rise for one hour. Make loaves and bake in greased bread pans which have been sprinkled with cornmeal. Bake in 375 degree oven about 35 minutes.

Sudie's Meltaway Rolls

Ingredients:

  2 cups dry curd cottage cheese
  1/2 lb. plus 2 Tbsps. butter
  2/3 cup plus 1 Tbsp. flour
  1 8-oz. pkg. cream cheese
  2 egg yolks, beaten

In a blender, process cottage cheese. Add flour and 1/2 pound of the butter until well blended. Refrigerate overnight.

When ready to prepare rolls, roll dough into two circles each about ten inches in diameter; dough will be thin. Cut each circle into pie shaped wedges.

Mix cream cheese, egg yolks and two tablespoons of the butter together. Spread mixture on the wedges. Roll up wedges, starting from wide end.

Place on a greased baking sheet. Refrigerate 30 minutes before baking.

Bake in 400 degree oven for 25 minutes.

These are good frozen and reheated.

Sudie, my Kentucky friend, sent me this recipe especially for this cookbook. These rolls are good served as either dinner rolls or as breakfast rolls.

At lunch, they are especially good with a casserole and a salad.

For a sweet roll, add these ingredients to the cream cheese filling:

1/2 cup sugar
1 t. cinnamon
1/2 t. vanilla

These rolls can also be served as hors d'oeuvres; just add these ingredients to the cream cheese filling:

1 small can deviled ham
1/2 t. horseradish

Serve with this dip alongside:

1/2 cup mayonnaise
1/2 cup sour cream
1 t. horseradish

Six-Weeks Bran Muffins

Ingredients:
>1 15-oz. box Raisin Bran
>3 cups sugar
>5 cups flour
>5 tsps. soda
>2 tsps. salt
>5 beaten eggs
>1 cup corn oil
>4 cups buttermilk

Mix together Raisin Bran, sugar, flour, soda and salt. Add beaten eggs, corn oil and buttermilk.

Mix well. Store in a covered container in the refrigerator. Use as needed. As the name indicates, this mixture will keep well for about six weeks in the refrigerator.

To bake:
Fill greased muffin tins two-thirds full and bake at 400 degrees until done, about 12-15 minutes.

These can also be baked in a microwave for three minutes at 50% power for six muffins (or for 2-1/2 minutes on high). Rotate muffins halfway through cooking. They will appear doughy on top, but they continue cooking after they are taken from oven.

If baking muffins in the microwave, you can use recycled plastic ice cream cups as muffin dishes. After using, they can be saved for reuse or discarded. The plastic cups can also be lined with muffin papers for convenience.

Corn Cups

Ingredients:
- **1/2 cup butter, softened**
- **1 3-oz. pkg. cream cheese, softened**
- **1 cup flour**
- **1 cup cornmeal**
- **1/2 tsp. salt**

This is extra good when filled with the stew from the recipe on page 39.

Cream butter and cream cheese together.

Combine flour, cornmeal and salt. Add these dry ingredients a little at a time to butter mixture, stirring continually until well mixed.

Divide dough into small balls. Place a ball in each compartment of a greased muffin tin. Press each dough ball onto the bottom and sides of a muffin compartment until the dough lines the tin, forming individual cups.

Bake at 350 degrees for 20 minutes.

Remove from pan and will with hot stew, chili or creamed vegetables.

Desserts

Desserts

This special collection of dessert recipes has been gathered from the files of the best cooks I know. Only those recipes that are seldom found today have been included. Many of the recipes are old family gems which never fail to bring compliments to the cook. I feel fortunate that so many cooks were willing to share recipes from their private collections and feel sure that you, too, will be asked to share the recipes.

I've included several recipes which call for mincemeat made from game meat, since these recipes are both delicious and hard to find. Gourmet Game Mincemeat has a wonderful flavor and is nourishing. Many of these mincemeat recipes have been developed especially to be made from game meat, although they are also good with beef. The dessert possibilities for Gourmet Game Mincemeat are unending; make your own masterpiece with this versatile dessert ingredient.

Pineapple Fudge

Ingredients:

   3 cups sugar
   1 small can crushed pineapple
   1 cup canned milk
   1 cup white syrup
   1/4 tsp. cream of tartar
   1/4 cup butter
   1 cup chopped nuts

Drain pineapple.

In three-quart saucepan, mix together sugar, white syrup, pineapple, milk and cream of tartar. Cook over medium heat until a drop of cooked mixture forms a good soft ball when dropped into cold water.

Remove from heat; add butter and nuts.

Let stand five minutes. Beat and pour into a 9-inch square, buttered pan.

Let cool until set before serving.

Caramel Nut Pie

Ingredients:

1 packet unflavored gelatin
1/4 cup cold water
1/2 lb. vanilla caramels
3/4 cup milk
1 cup cream, whipped
1 cup chopped nuts
1 graham cracker pie crust,
            prepared

You may substitute non-dairy frozen topping for whipped cream in this recipe and in most recipes. Frozen topping is best when just thawed and still very cold.

Soften gelatin in cold water. Melt caramels in milk in top of double boiler. Add softened gelatin and stir well.

Chill until partially thickened; then add whipped cream and nuts.

Pour mixture into graham cracker crust and chill.

Garnish with chopped nuts and more whipped cream.

Bernice's Blueberry Favorite

Ingredients:

- 1/4 lb. vanilla wafers
- 3/4 cup sugar, divided
- 1/2 cup butter, softened
- 2 eggs, slightly beaten
- 1 8-oz. pkg. cream cheese, softened
- 1 tsp. vanilla
- 1 can blueberries
- 1 tsp. lemon juice
- 2 tsps. cornstarch

This makes a great dessert for wedding showers and special get-togethers.

Crust:

Crush vanilla wafers; mix in soft butter and 1/4 cup of the sugar. Line baking dish with wafer mixture and bake for ten minutes in a 350 degree oven. Cool.

First layer:

Combine eggs, cream cheese, 1/2 cup of the sugar, and vanilla. Beat together until smooth. Pour over crust. Bake for 15 minutes in 375 degree oven. Cool.

Top layer:

Combine blueberries, lemon juice and cornstarch and cook on stovetop until thickened. Cool; then spread over baked cream cheese layer.

Refrigerate until ready to serve.

Choconut Pie

This recipe is really best with real whipping cream, rather than frozen non-dairy whipped topping. It is luscious!

Ingredients:

3/4 cup butter, melted
1 1/2 cup graham cracker crumbs
3 Tbsps. sugar
1/4 cup creamy peanut butter
1 can prepared chocolate frosting
1 3/4 cups whipping cream
1/2 cup chopped salted peanuts

Mix melted butter, graham cracker crumbs, sugar, and peanut butter together. Line bottom and sides of 9-inch pie pan with crumb mixture. Bake crust in 350 degree oven for ten minutes. Let cool.

To make filling, beat together whipping cream and the can of chocolate frosting. Beat until thick and fluffy.

Fold salted peanuts into filling mixture.

Pour filling into crust and garnish with more chopped peanuts.

Freeze until firm.

Earl's Orange Dream

Ingredients:

2 1/2 cups peeled, chopped oranges
1/2 cup plus 1/3 cup sugar
1 cup crushed Rice Chex cereal
1/4 cup firmly-packed brown sugar
1/2 tsp. ginger, divided
1/3 cup butter, melted
2 Tbsps. cornstarch
1 3-oz pkg. cream cheese, softened
orange juice
1 Tbsp. milk

Earl traveled around the world collecting recipes. This one he found in the southern part of the U.S. and gave me permission to use it in this book.

First mix chopped oranges together with 1/2 cup of the sugar. Set mixture aside to allow it to make syrup.

Shredded coconut is a nice garnish for this dessert.

To make crust, combine Rice Chex, brown sugar, 1/4 teaspoon of the ginger, and butter. Press into bottom and sides of a 9-inch pie pan. Preheat oven to 350 degrees and bake for ten minutes.

To make sauce, combine cornstarch and 1/3 cup of the sugar. Drain syrup from chopped oranges and add enough orange juice to the syrup to make one cup. Stir orange juice into sugar mixture. Cook over low heat, stirring, until thick and clear. Cool.

Combine cream cheese, milk and remaining 1/4 teaspoon of ginger. Spread cream cheese mixture on bottom and sides of pie shell. Stir orange pieces into sauce and pour into crust. Chill.

Margaret's Brandy Alexander Souffle

Ingredients:
- 1 packet unflavored gelatin
- 1 cup skimmed milk, divided
- 4 eggs, separated
- 1/3 cup sugar
- 1/8 tsp. salt
- 2 Tbsps. brandy
- 2 Tbsps. creme de cacao

Soften gelatin in 1/2 cup of the cold milk in top of double boiler. Do not heat; just soften.

In a bowl, beat together egg yolks, salt, and remaining 1/2 cup of milk. Add this to gelatin mixture in double boiler and cook over boiling water, stirring constantly until gelatin dissolves and mixture mounds slightly when dropped from spoon. Cool; then carefully fold in brandy and creme de cacao.

Beat egg whites until stiff; gradually add sugar and beat until very stiff.

Fold whipped egg whites into cooled gelatin mixture. Turn out into four-cup souffle dish. Chill until set.

CHERRY BRANDIED APPLES

3 tart apples
1 1/2 cups cherry - flavored brandy
1/2 cup butter
Powdered sugar

Peel, core and slice apples. Marinate apples in brandy for three hours.

Drain apples and dust with flour. Then saute apples in fry pan in 1/2 cup of butter until brown. Dust with powdered sugar.

Frosty Lime

Ingredients:

    2 cups of ginger snap cookies
    1 6-oz. can frozen limeade, thawed
    1 can Eagle Brand condensed milk
    1 quart non-dairy frozen topping
    1 packet unflavored gelatin
    1 cup water, divided

Crust:

Crush ginger snap cookies to crumbs. Pat one cup of crumbs into bottom of an 8-by-10 inch pan. Save remaining crumbs for garnish.

Filling:

Soften gelatin in 1/4 cup of the water. Heat remaining 3/4 cup water to boiling and add to gelatin, stirring until dissolved.

Mix limeade, topping, and Eagle Brand sweetened condensed milk (add a dash of green food coloring, if you desire). Add gelatin/water mixture to topping mixture and stir. Pour filling over crumb crust. Sprinkle remaining crumbs over top and chill until set.

This pie can also be made with frozen lemonade for a variation. Use pink lemonade plus a little red food coloring to get a different coloration.

Vanilla wafers substitute well for the ginger snaps.

Peanut Butter Pie

This recipe comes from the files of Helen, a wonderful cook, who feeds many ranch hands year around.

Ingredients:
1 baked 9-inch pie crust
1 packet unflavored gelatin
1/2 cup sugar, divided
1 cup milk
2 eggs, separated
2/3 cup smooth peanut butter
1 cup sour cream

In top of a double boiler, mix gelatin and 1/4 cup of the sugar. Add milk and egg yolks; beat until blended. Cook over boiling water until mixture is slightly thickened.

Remove from heat and transfer to bowl. Beat in peanut butter and then allow to cool thoroughly.

Beat egg whites until stiff, gradually adding the remaining 1/4 cup sugar.

Stir sour cream into cooked peanut butter mixture. Lastly, fold in egg whites.

Pour filling into pie shell and chill until firm.

May be topped with vanilla ice cream or whipped cream.

Sourdough Chocolate Cake

Ingredients:
- **1 1/2 cups sugar**
- **2/3 cup butter**
- **3 eggs**
- **1 cup sourdough starter (P. 112))**
- **1 3/4 cups flour**
- **1/2 cup cocoa**
- **1/2 tsp. baking powder**
- **1/4 tsp. salt**
- **1 tsp. cinnamon**
- **1/2 tsp. ground cloves**
- **3/4 cup water**
- **1 1/2 tsps. soda**
- **2 tsps. vanilla**

A sourdough starter recipe and several recipes for delicious sourdough breads can be found in the bread section of this cookbook.

Cream together sugar and butter. Add eggs and beat thoroughly. Add sourdough starter and blend together.

Sift together flour, cocoa, baking powder, salt, cinnamon and cloves. Add vanilla to water; dissolve soda in vanilla/water mixture. Alternately add water mixture and dry ingredients to starter mixture.

Pour into greased 9-x-13 inch pan and bake in 350 degree oven for 30 minutes.

Rhubarb Crunch

Try eating this warm with a scoop of homemade vanilla ice cream on top.

Ingredients:
- 1 cup all purpose flour
- 1/2 cup melted butter
- 1 tsp. cinnamon
- 3/4 cup oatmeal
- 1 cup brown sugar
- 4 cups of chopped rhubarb
- 1 cup sugar
- 1 cup water
- 2 Tbsps. cornstarch
- 1 tsp. vanilla

Crust:
Mix together flour, melted butter, cinnamon, oatmeal and brown sugar. Pat half of mixture into 9-x-12 inch baking dish; save remaining crumbs for topping.

Filling:
Cover crust with chopped rhubarb. Cook sugar, water and cornstarch together until sugar dissolves. Take mixture from burner and add vanilla. Pour this sauce over rhubarb.

Cover rhubarb with remaining crumb mixture.

Bake at 350 degrees for one hour.

Pear Chocolate Upside-down Cake

Ingredients:

- **7 Tbsps. butter**
- **3/4 cup brown sugar, packed**
- **2 Tbsps. corn syrup**
- **1 1/4 cups flaked coconut**
- **8 canned pear halves, drained**
- **1 1/2 cups flour**
- **1 tsp. baking powder**
- **1 tsp. soda**
- **1/4 cup cocoa**
- **1 cup sugar**
- **2 slightly beaten eggs**
- **1 cup sour cream**
- **1 tsp. vanilla**

If you are seeking an unusual, attractive and delicious dessert, I suggest this one.

Pear layer:

In 9-x-9-x-2 inch baking pan, melt butter. Remove from heat. Stir in brown sugar, corn syrup and coconut. Pat evenly over bottom and sides of pan. Place pear halves on top and chill.

Cake layer:

Combine flour, baking powder, soda, cocoa, and sugar. Add eggs, sour cream and vanilla. Pour this cake layer over chilled pear layer.

Bake in preheated oven at 375 degrees for 35 minutes, or until done. Let cool for five minutes before removing from pan. Turn upside down on a serving platter. Serve warm.

White Chocolate Mousse

Ingredients:

7-oz. white chocolate, melted
6 large eggs, separated
2 level Tbsps. plus 1 tsp. sugar
13-oz whipping cream

Chop chocolate very fine. Place it in small bowl over larger bowl of very hot water. Stir until it is smooth and melted. Be very careful not to let it get too hot as the milk solids will lump.

Whip egg yolks to a ribbon, about five minutes, with an electric mixer.

In a separate bowl whip egg whites until soft peaks form; then begin adding sugar until all sugar is added. Beat until stiff.

In another bowl beat whipping cream to medium soft peaks.

Quickly combine ingredients. This takes fast work to assure a smooth mousse. Quickly whisk melted chocolate into egg yolks, using a hand whisk. Speed is most important. If added too slowly it will solidify, and there will be chips of chocolate in the mousse.

Next fold in egg whites, being gentle enough not to deflate mixture. Then fold in whipped cream.

Chill for two hours before serving.

This mousse is a speciality of Dessert Chef Rebecca Barnhart. Her desserts have pleased patrons of San Francisco and Denver restaurants and this one will please your guests. I serve this mousse regularly; it is not hard to make if the directions are carefully followed.

This may be served with fresh berries for that special dinner.

This mousse is also good flavored with either Grand Marnier or white rum.

Molasses Cake

Ingredients:

- **1/2 cup butter**
- **1 cup sugar**
- **1/2 cup molasses**
- **1 egg**
- **1/2 cup milk**
- **2 cups flour**
- **2 tsps. baking powder**
- **1/4 tsp. salt**
- **1/2 tsp. baking soda**
- **1 tsp. cinnamon**
- **1 tsp. ginger**
- **1/2 tsp. cloves**
- **1/2 cup raisins (optional)**

This 100-year-old recipe was shared by Grace Mueller. It has been handed down through the generations of the Mueller family and came to Wyoming by way of Illinois.

Cream butter and sugar; stir in molasses and egg.

Sift flour with other dry ingredients. Alternately add dry mixture and milk to butter mixture. Beat after each addition until well blended. Add raisins, if desired.

Pour into a buttered, floured 9-by-13 inch pan or into two layer cake pans.

Bake in 350 degree oven for 30-35 minutes.

Frost with white icing or serve with whipped cream.

Raisin Pudding

Ingredients:
- 1 1/2 cups milk
- 3 eggs
- 1/4 tsp. nutmeg
- 1 tsp. cinnamon
- 2 Tbsps. melted butter
- 1/4 cup molasses
- 1/4 cup brown sugar
- 1 cups raisins
- 1 cup graham cracker crumbs

Blend milk, eggs, nutmeg, cinnamon, butter, molasses and brown sugar together in a blender Blend until smooth.

Add raisins and blend two seconds.

Add graham cracker crumbs and blend only long enough to mix.

Pour into a well-greased loaf pan. Bake at 375 degrees for 40 minutes.

Best Ever Mincemeat

Ingredients:

    3 quarts boiled Gourmet Game Meat, ground fine
    1 quart dark molasses
    1 quart lemon juice
    2 quarts raisins
    1/2 pound butter
    1 Tbsp. salt
    3 quarts sugar
    5 quarts chopped apples
    3 lemons, grind together with peels and juice
    1 small orange, grind together with peels and juice
    2 Tbsps. cinnamon
    2 Tbsps. nutmeg
    2 Tbsps. cloves

Mix all together except meat and cinnamon, nutmeg and cloves. Boil until apples are tender. Then add meat and spices. Mix well and can or freeze.

Will keep in a glass container in bottom of refrigerator for up to one year.

This is the primary ingredient of many fine dessert recipes.

I freeze this mincemeat in one-quart, plastic containers to use as I need it. It never freezes completely solid so the amount needed can easily be spooned out of the container. Do make sure that the lids are on tightly because the mincemeat will spill if tipped over in the freezer.

Mincemeat Bars

Ingredients:
- **2 1/2 cups flour**
- **1/2 tsp. salt**
- **1 cup butter**
- **1 egg, separated**
- **2/3 cup milk**
- **2 cups mincemeat** (see p. 143)
- **1 Tbsp. brandy flavoring**

Brandy flavoring can be found in the spice department of supermarkets. Sometimes I substitute 1 t. of real brandy and 1 t. of rum flavoring for the brandy flavoring.

Add brandy flavoring to mincemeat and set aside.

Mix flour, salt, and butter. Mix egg yolk and milk; add to flour mixture. Blend well. Divide dough into two portions. Roll one portion of dough to fit cookie sheet with one inch to turn back at edges. Spread mincemeat over dough. Roll other half of dough to cover top. Seal edges and cut slits in top. Brush tops with egg white.

Bake in 400 degree oven for 30 minutes. Cool and frost with powdered sugar frosting (see p. 117). Cut into squares.

Mincemeat Diamonds

Ingredients:

- **2 cups flour**
- **1 1/2 cups oatmeal**
- **3/4 cup brown sugar**
- **1 cup butter**
- **1 3-oz. pkg. cream cheese, softened**
- **1/2 cup sour cream**
- **2 eggs**
- **2 cups moist mincemeat** (see p. 143)
- **1/2 cup chopped walnuts**

This is a delicately-flavored bar cookie suitable for the holidays or perfect to serve with afternoon tea.

Crust:

Mix flour, oatmeal, brown sugar and butter together until it resembles coarse meal. Press three-quarters of this crumb mixture around the bottom and sides of 9-x-13 inch baking dish.

Filling:

Beat together cream cheese, sour cream and eggs. Stir in mincemeat.

Pour the filling into unbaked crust. Spread remaining oatmeal mixture over top of mincemeat mixture. Top with chopped walnuts.

Bake in 350 degree oven for 30 minutes. Cut into diamonds while still warm.

Mincemeat Stuffed Apples

Ingredients:

    6 large, tart apples, cored
    1 1/2 cup mincemeat (see p. 143)
    1/2 cup brown sugar
    1 Tbsp. lemon juice

Core the apples. Fill each apple with about two tablespoons of mincemeat.

Heat brown sugar and lemon juice in a saucepan, stirring constantly, until it is syrupy.

Pour syrup into bottom of baking pan. Set in filled apples. Baste apples with syrup occasionally while baking.

Bake in 350 degree oven until apples are tender, about 45 minutes.

Diana's Jiffy Mince Cake

Ingredients:

2 cups flour
3/4 cup sugar
2 1/2 tsp. baking powder
1/3 cup shortening
1 egg
1/2 cup milk
3/4 cup moist mincemeat (see p.143)

Sift together flour, sugar, and baking powder. Cut in shortening, until mixture is crumbly:

Beat egg and milk together. Blend mincemeat into milk/egg mixture.

Add mincemeat mixture to dry ingredients and mix only until flour is moistened. Turn into well-greased and floured 9-inch baking pan.

Bake in 350 degree oven for 30 minutes.

Coffee frosting is especially good on this cake.

COFFEE
FROSTING

1/4 cup butter.
1/2 cup brown
*   sugar (packed)*
3 T. milk.
1 t. instant coffee
*   powder,*
1 t. vanilla
Powdered sugar

In small saucepan over medium heat, melt butter. Add brown sugar and milk.
Bring to a boil, stirring constantly, for one minute. Remove from heat. Add coffee powder and vanilla. Mix well.

Sift powdered sugar and add enough so that frosting is of spreading consistency.

Mary's Mince Pudding

This dessert tastes equally scrumptious when poured into a baked pie shell, a graham cracker crust or a cornflake crust.

Ingredients:

1 pkg. instant vanilla pudding mix
3/4 cup milk
1/2 cup sour cream
1 cup moist mincemeat (see p. 143)
1 8-oz. container non-dairy
    whipped topping
1 9-inch crumb crust
candied cherries

Combine pudding mix and milk. Beat. Add sour cream and mincemeat (Gourmet game mincemeat works well; see recipe on page 143) Mix well. Blend in thawed topping.

Spoon into crust and garnish with chopped, candied cherries. Chill several hours before serving.

This delightful dessert will make a hit with mincemeat lovers and with the uninitiated as well.

Field Care
& Aging

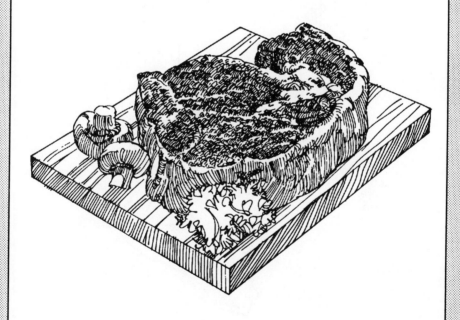

Cuts of Meat

*Thanks to
Evelyn Williams
for this illustration.*

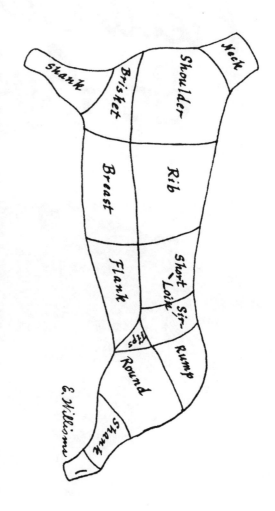

Big Game Animals - Basic Cuts

Field Care & Aging of Game

Field care and aging make all the difference in the flavor of game.

The first and most important step to edible game meat is proper dressing in the field. The meat should be cleaned, cooled and the scent glands should be removed immediately to preserve flavor.

As soon as possible, all hair and dirt should be removed. Before freezing, remove as much fat as possible.

Many practical considerations must determine whether to age game meat or not. Among these are the temperature and relative humidity at the time of the kill, the chilling rate, the internal temperature of the muscle after chilling, the youthfulness of the animal, the amount of meat the hunter is willing to sacrifice, the processing procedure, and, if the animal is going to be processed commercially, the amount of cooler space and labor available.

Aging game meat usually results in improvement in tenderness and flavor, but aging carcasses with little or no fat cover is not recommended by specialists. These carcasses lose moisture quickly, resulting in excessive weight loss and surface discoloration of lean meats. Also aged meat with little fat is exposed and susceptible to deterioration through microbial growth.

Meat that is to be ground or made into sausages need not be aged because grinding and chopping tenderize the meat.

The decision whether or not to age game meat can be made easier by understanding the changes which occur during the aging period. Immediately after the kill, the meat decreases in tenderness. This is because the muscles shorten and harden. After the third day, meat which has been cooled at 30 degrees Fahrenheit has returned to the original tenderness level.

If the carcass is to be cut into chops, steaks and roasts, additional aging is often recommended. If stored at 34 degrees Fahrenheit and high humidity, bacterial growth will not develop on the meat until after the fourteenth day. This, along with the fact that tenderization proceeds more slowly after the fourteenth day of aging, is the reason that aging should be limited to a maximum of two weeks.

Many meat processors do not recommend aging game. Their reasoning is that much of the game delivered to a processor has already been aged long enough. If the game carcass could not be chilled after the kill, then the aging process is often quickened by the increased temperature. This is because the activity of natural enzymes, which are responsible for the meat's tenderness, increases at higher temperatures.

The temperature at the time of the kill

also affects the aging recommendations. A 65 degree temperature at the time of the kill will result in less toughening and hardening of the muscles than will occur if the temperature is cooler.

Therefore, the resulting tenderization is the same if an animal is killed when the temperature is 65 degrees and aged for three days at that temperature or if the more conventional aging process of 34 degrees for two weeks is used.

Game slaughtered during the cold months of November and December should be aged longer than that harvested in the warm months of September and October because alternating day and night temperatures speed up the aging process. Under alternating temperatures, aging game meat one week or less is recommended.

During warm hunting seasons, special field care is a must to keep carcasses cool and clean. Store the meat in the shade and wrap it in cheesecloth or lightweight cotton bags. Do not wrap meat in airtight game bags or heavy tarps. These trap the heat and cause rapid spoilage.

Antelope carcasses should be cut and wrapped for the freezer within three days of the kill. This short aging period helps prevent the "liver-like" or "mushy" texture sometimes found in this meat.

Field Care & Aging of Game

Deer, sheep, goat, cow elk and cow moose carcasses should be cut within seven days of the kill, if the meat has been held at temperatures higher than 40 degrees Fahrenheit.

Bull elk and moose carcasses need a longer aging period for proper tenderization. They should be cut after aging for fourteen days at 34-37 degrees Fahrenheit.

Here are some good general rules:

- Do not age any game carcass which was shot during warm weather and not chilled rapidly.
- Do not age any animal which was severely stressed prior to the kill.
- Do not age if the gunshot wounds are extensive.
- Do not age if the animal was under one year old.
- Aging has already occurred if the carcass has been in camp for one week in relatively warm weather; no further aging is recommended.

Decisions concerning the aging process are important to the resulting flavor and tenderness of the meat. Although many variables exist, a person with an understanding of the aging process can make an informed decision which results in game meat which can be used deliciously in any recipe.

Index

Aging
General 151-154
Pheasant.....................44

Beets .....(see Vegetables)
Breads
Biscuit Mix.................37
Corn Cups 125
Cornmeal Buns.......120
Dough for Deep-Fried
Sandwiches..............51
Lithuanian Rye 122
Muffins, Bran 124
Quiche Crust 42
Rolls
Herbed 119
Oatmeal 121
Meltaway, Sudie's 123
Potato 118
Rye, Lithuanian 122
Saffron......................117
Sourdough
Biscuits...................113
Cake.........................137
Date Loaf 115
Pancakes.................114
Starter.....................112
Tortillas.....................36
Yam 116
Broccoli (see Vegetables)
Burger (see Gourmet
Grind)

Cabbage (see Vegetables)
Cake
Mince, Jiffy...............147
Molasses...................141
Pear Chocolate
Upside-Down.......139

Cake (continued)
Sourdough...............137
Candy
Pineapple Fudge 129
Carrots..(see Vegetables)
Celery ...(see Vegetables)
Chops
Caramelized with Wal-
nuts & Raisins.........21
with Cabbage 23
Glazed 24
in Wine Sauce............22
Crepes, Stuffed............31
Corn ......(see Vegetables)
Cuts, Illustrated........150

Desserts (see also cake,
pie, mincemeat)
Apples, Brandied ...134
Brandy Alexander
Souffle 134
Mousse, White
Chocolate...............140
Raisin Pudding.......142
Rhubarb Crunch.....138
Dip .... (see Sauce)
Duck ...(see Fowl, Wild)

Equivalents
Pasta, etc....................80
Sausage Seasonings .68

Field Care of Wild
Game.................151-154
Fish
Trout, Canned......76-77
Fowl, Wild
Duck
with Stuffing 47

Index

Fowl, Duck (continued)
   Roast, Glazed...........48
   Pheasant
     in Casserole..............45
     Curried......................46
     in Sour Cream Gravy 44
   Turkey
     Smoked Wild..........49
Frosting
   Powdered Sugar.....117
   Coffee.........................147
Fudge...........(see Candy)

Gameburger.............(see
   Gourmet Grind)
Gourmet Grind
   Basic Seasoning.........34
   Ground Meat Jerky ..60
   Gourmet Tart.............37
   Jalapenos Treat..........35
   Meatballs....................38
   Meximix......................41
   Quiche.......................42
   Sour Cream Chili Bake.36
   Taco Teaser.................40
Gravy............(see Sauce)
Grits......(see Vegetables)

Hamburger...............(see
   Gourmet Grind)
Harvest Feast...............14
Holiday Buffet.............14

Ice Bowl........................29

Jerky
   Dry Cured..................56
   from Dry Cured Meat ..61
   Ground Meat.............60

Jerky (continued)
   Gourmet.....................63
   Hunters'......................62
   Introduction to 54-55
   Marinated..................59
   Pickle Cured..............57
   Pickle Cured, Hot.....58

Meat (see chops, fowl,
   Gourmet Grind, jerky,
   mincemeat, roast,
   sausage, steaks)
   Cooking Tips........12-13
Meat, Sliced/Chunked
   Barbecue....................50
   Deep-Fried
     Sandwiches...........51
   Gourmet Parmesan..25
   Jerky Strips ..(see jerky)
   Stew, Gourmet..........39
   Strips with Noodles
     & Sour Cream......26
Menu Suggestions.....14
Mincemeat
   Apples Stuffed with.146
   Basic Recipe.............143
   Best Ever...................143
   Bars............................144
   Cake...........................147
   Diamonds.................145
   Pudding....................148

New Year's Supper....14

Onions (see Vegetables)

Pheasant........(see Fowl)
Pie
   Blueberry Favorite .131

Index

Pie (continued
  Caramel Nut............130
  Choconut 132
  Orange Dream 133
  Lime, Frosty.............135
  Peanut Butter 136
Potatoes(see Vegetables)

Quiche
  Crust 42
  South of the Border..42
  Summer Sausage......52

Rhubarb (see Vegetables)
Roasts
  Another Moist...........27
  Moist Perfection........27
  Chopped/Sliced Roast
    Curried.....................28
    Crepes, Stuffed 31
    Mousse, Elegant.....30
    Salad, Luncheon.....29
    Tomato Baskets 43
    Turnovers 32
Rolls ....(see Bread)

Salad
  Cream Slaw 105
  Cucumber/Pineapple
   106
  Cucumber 106
  Fruit Slaw.................103
  Molded
    Aspic 100
    Avocado/Grapefruit
   102
    Bean, Kidney 102
    Beet............................99
    Cranberry..............104

Salad
  Molded (continued)
    Festive Salad 104
    Gelatin, Softening ..30
    Grapefruit..............102
    Meat Salads
      Luncheon 29
      Mousse 30
    Vegetable, Mixed .101
  Orange Salad...........103
  Rhubarb 107

Salami ......(see Sausage)
Sauce
  Bacon-Cheese............51
  Cream Sauce.............24
  Horseradish Dip.......16
  Mushroom Gravy.....15
  Thickening Gravy 19
  Salsa, Easy.................35
  Wild Plum Dressing.33
Sausage
  Basics 64
  Bockwurst.................74
  Casings 67
  Cures..........................65
  Equipment 66
  Equivalents................68
  Fresh 69
  Liver...........................70
  Polish 72
  Thuringer 71
  Salami 73
  Summer Sausage......75
Steak
  Chicken Fried............16
  Gourmet Delight 18
  with Honey Sauce 20
  Rolls Roices...............19

Index

Steak (continued)
Royal Stuffed............15
Tarragon Cube 17
Sweet Potatoes (see Veg.)
Tomatoes (see Vegetables)
Trout ....(see Fish)
Turkey (see Fowl, Wild)

Vegetables
Beets
New York 93
Salad.........................99
in Sauce....................93
Broccoli
Best 89
Souffle 90
Cabbage
Cream Slaw...........102
with Chops..............23
in Potato Sauce 88
Carrots
Sweet and Sour 92
Surprise....................91
Celery/Mushroom
Treat...........................87
Corn
Bake...........................96
Sylvia's CC 98
Cucumber
Another Salad.......106
with Pineapple 106
Grits Elegant.............97
Onions
a la Dee 86
Saucy.........................85
Potatoes
Dumplings..............83
Julie...........................82
Rolls.........................118

Vegetables (continued)
Rhubarb
Crunch 138
Salad.......................107
Sweet Potatoes 84
Tomatoes
Baskets 43
Broiled......................95
Pudding...................31
Scalloped 94
Yam Bread................116
Zucchini 25

Wine, Suggestions 80

Yams .....(see Vegetables)

Zucchini (see Vegetables)

Game in Good Taste
High Plains Press
P.O. Box 123
Glendo, WY 82213

| Standard Trade |
| Discounts Available |
| to Retailers |

Send me _____copies of the cookbook at $9.95 each, plus $1.25 per book for shipping. Wyoming residents add 30 cents per book for sales tax.

Name_____

Address_____

City/State/Zip_____

Enclosed is my check for $_____payable to High Plains Press.

Game in Good Taste
High Plains Press
P.O. Box 123
Glendo, WY 82213

| Standard Trade |
| Discounts Available |
| to Retailers |

Send me _____copies of the cookbook at $9.95 each, plus $1.25 per book for shipping. Wyoming residents add 30 cents per book for sales tax.

Name_____

Address_____

City/State/Zip_____

Enclosed is my check for $_____payable to High Plains Press.

Game in Good Taste
High Plains Press
P.O. Box 123
Glendo, WY 82213

| Standard Trade |
| Discounts Available |
| to Retailers |

Send me _____copies of the cookbook at $9.95 each, plus $1.25 per book for shipping. Wyoming residents add 30 cents per book for sales tax.

Name_____

Address_____

City/State/Zip_____

Enclosed is my check for $_____payable to High Plains Press.